Entity Framework Tutorial

Learn to build a better data access layer with the ADO.NET Entity Framework and ADO.NET Data Services

Joydip Kanjilal

BIRMINGHAM - MUMBAI

Entity Framework Tutorial

Copyright © 2008 Packt Publishing

All rights reserved. No part of this book may be reproduced, stored in a retrieval system, or transmitted in any form or by any means, without the prior written permission of the publisher, except in the case of brief quotations embedded in critical articles or reviews.

Every effort has been made in the preparation of this book to ensure the accuracy of the information presented. However, the information contained in this book is sold without warranty, either express or implied. Neither the author, Packt Publishing, nor its dealers or distributors will be held liable for any damages caused or alleged to be caused directly or indirectly by this book.

Packt Publishing has endeavored to provide trademark information about all the companies and products mentioned in this book by the appropriate use of capitals. However, Packt Publishing cannot guarantee the accuracy of this information.

First published: October 2008

Production Reference: 1201008

Published by Packt Publishing Ltd.
32 Lincoln Road
Olton
Birmingham, B27 6PA, UK.

ISBN 978-1-847195-22-7

www.packtpub.com

Cover Image by Vinayak Chittar (vinayak.chittar@gmail.com)

Credits

Author
Joydip Kanjilal

Reviewers
Bogdan Brinzarea-Iamandi
Stefan Turalski

Senior Acquisition Editor
Douglas Paterson

Development Editor
Ved Prakash Jha

Technical Editor
Ajay Shanker

Editorial Team Leader
Mithil Kulkarni

Project Manager
Abhijeet Deobhakta

Project Coordinator
Lata Basantani

Indexer
Monica Ajmera

Proofreader
Joel T. Johnson

Production Coordinator
Aparna Bhagat

Cover Work
Aparna Bhagat

About the Author

Joydip Kanjilal is a Microsoft MVP in ASP.NET. He has over 12 years of industry experience in IT with more than 6 years in Microsoft .NET and its related technologies. He has authored many articles for some of the most reputable sites like, `www.asptoday.com`, `www.devx.com`, `www.aspalliance.com`, `www.aspnetpro.com`, `www.sql-server-performance.com`, `www.sswug.com`, etc. Several of these articles have been featured at `www.asp.net` — Microsoft's Official Site on ASP.NET. Joydip was also a community credit winner at `www.community-credit.com` a number of times.

He is currently working as a Senior Consultant in a reputable company in Hyderabad, INDIA. He has years of experience in designing and architecting solutions for various domains. His technical strengths include C, C++, VC++, Java, C#, Microsoft .NET, Ajax, Design Patterns, SQL Server, Operating Systems, and Computer Architecture. Joydip blogs at `http://aspadvice.com/blogs/joydip` and spends most of his time reading books, blogs, and writing books and articles. His hobbies include watching cricket and soccer and playing chess.

> Writing a book is always a rewarding experience. My special thanks to Douglas Paterson for providing me the opportunity to author this book — turning this idea into a reality. I am also thankful to the entire Packt team for their support.
>
> I am also thankful to Abhishek Kant (Microsoft), Steve Smith (AspAlliance), Russell Jones(DevX), Steve Jones(SSWUG), Jude Kelly (SQL Server Performance), and Anand Narayaswamy (AspAlliance) for their inspiration and support. My heartiest thanks to my friends Tilak and Vinod for their continued encouragement.
>
> My deepest respects and gratitude to my parents for their love, blessings, and encouragement. My thanks to my other family members too, for their support, and to little Jini in particular, for her continued inspiration and love.
>
> Thank you all so much!

About the Reviewer

Bogdan Brinzarea-Iamandi has a strong background in Computer Science holding a Master and Bachelor Degree at the Automatic Control and Computers Faculty of the Politehnica University of Bucharest, Romania. He also holds an Auditor diploma at the Computer Science department at Ecole Polytechnique, Paris, France. His main interests cover a wide area from embedded programming, distributed and mobile computing, and new web technologies.

Currently, he is employed as Supervisor within the team of Alternative Channels Sector of the IT Division in Banca Romaneasca, a Member of the National Bank of Greece. He is Project Manager for Internet Banking and he coordinates other projects related to new technologies and applications to be implemented within the banking area.

Bogdan is also the author of two AJAX books, the popular AJAX and PHP: Building Responsive Web Applications and Microsoft AJAX Library Essentials, also by Packt.

Table of Contents

Preface	**1**
Chapter 1: Introducing the ADO.NET Entity Framework	**7**
What You should Know	8
Looking Back	8
What is ADO.NET Entity Framework?	9
Is It Just Another ORM?	9
The ADO.NET Entity Framework Architectural Components	10
The Entity Data Model (EDM)	10
How is the Entity Data Model Represented?	13
The Object Model (O-Space)	15
LINQ to Entities	15
Entity Client	16
Entity SQL	16
Avoiding Complex Joins	17
The Object Services Layer	18
ADO.NET Entity Framework—Features and Benefits at a Glance	19
Installing the Prerequisites	20
Installing the ADO.NET Entity Framework and Its Tools	20
Downloading the Software	20
Installing the Software	21
Designing the Payroll Database	29
Summary	35
Glossary	35
Chapter 2: Getting Started	**37**
Creating an Entity Data Model	37
Creating the Payroll Entity Data Model Using the ADO.NET Entity Data Model Designer	38
Creating the Payroll Data Model Using the EdmGen Tool	47
The ADO.NET Entity Data Source Control	51

Implementing Our First Application Using the Entity Framework	**54**
Summary	**57**
Chapter 3: Entities, Relationships, and the Entity Data Model	**59**
Entities, Entity Types, and Relationships in the ADO.NET Entity Data Model (EDM)	**59**
What is an Entity?	60
Defining Entity Sets in the Entity Data Model	60
Extending the Existing Entity Types to Create Derived Entity Types	61
Association Sets, Associations, Containment, and Multiplicity	62
What are Entity Containers?	63
Exploring the Payroll Entity Data Model	**64**
The Mapping Details Window	65
The Entity Model Browser	67
The Entity Data Model Layers	68
The CSDL Schema	69
The SSDL Schema	75
The MSL Schema	80
Summary	**84**
Chapter 4: Working with Stored Procedures in the Entity Data Model	**85**
Mapping Stored Procedures to Functions in the EDM	**85**
Mapping Create, Update, and Delete Functions to Entities in the EDM	89
Mapping the Association Sets Consistently	93
Mapping Stored Procedures with No Entity Set	99
Using Stored Procedures	**100**
Mapping Stored Procedures that Return Custom Entity Types	**101**
Summary	**102**
Chapter 5: Working with Entity Client and Entity SQL	**103**
An Overview of the Entity SQL Language	**104**
From Transact SQL (T-SQL) to Entity SQL (E-SQL)	104
Why Entity SQL When I Already have LINQ to Entities?	105
Features of Entity SQL	105
Operators in Entity SQL	106
Arithmetic Operators	106
Comparison Operators	107
Logical Operators	107
Reference Operators	108
Type Operators	108
Set Operators	108
Operator Precedence	109
Expressions in Entity SQL	109
Query Expressions in Entity SQL	109

Identifiers, Variables, Parameters, and Types in Entity SQL	110
Row	111
Collection	111
Reference	112
Canonical Functions in Entity SQL	113
Mathematical Functions	113
Aggregate Functions	113
String Functions	114
Bitwise Functions	114
Date and Time Functions	115
Data Paging Using Entity SQL	**115**
Working with the ADO.NET Entity Client	**116**
Let's Get into Action	117
Building the Connection String	117
Creating an Entity Connection	118
Opening the Connection	118
Executing Queries Using the Entity Command	119
Closing the Connection	121
Other Operations with Entity SQL	**123**
Inserting a Record Using Entity SQL	123
Inserting a Record with a Foreign Key Constraint	124
Retrieving Native SQL from EntityCommand	124
Transaction Management in Entity SQL	125
Summary	**126**
Chapter 6: Working with LINQ to Entities	**127**
Introducing LINQ	**127**
Why LINQ?	128
Understanding the LINQ Architecture	**128**
LINQ to XML	129
LINQ to SQL	129
LINQ to Objects	130
LINQ to Entities	131
Querying Data Using LINQ to Entities	131
LINQ to Entities and Entity Framework	131
Differences between LINQ to Entities and LINQ to SQL	132
Operators in LINQ	**133**
Aggregation	136
Projections	136
Ordering	137
Quantifiers	137
Restriction	138
Conversion	138
Element	139
Set	139
Querying Data Using LINQ	**140**

Expressions in LINQ to Entities	143
Constant Expressions	144
Comparison Expressions	144
Initializing Expressions	145
Null Comparisons	146
Navigation Properties	147
Immediate and Deferred Query Execution	148
Improving Performance with Compiled Queries	150
Summary	**150**
Chapter 7: Working with the Object Services Layer	**151**
What are Object Services?	**151**
Features at a Glance	153
A Quick Look at the ObjectContext Class in our Payroll EDM	153
Querying Data as in-Memory Objects	156
Adding, Modifying, and Deleting Objects	**156**
Attaching and Detaching Objects to and from the Object Context	**158**
Serializing and De-Serializing Entity Instances	**159**
Change Tracking and Identity Resolution Using ObjectContext	**161**
Implementing a Sample Application	162
Creating the Form	162
Implementing a Custom DataContext	164
How is This Accomplished?	167
Inheritance in the Entity Framework	**176**
Table per Hierarchy	176
Table per Type	177
Implementing Complex Types in the EDM	**180**
Summary	**181**
Chapter 8: Introducing ADO.NET Data Services	**183**
Introducing ADO.NET Data Services	**184**
How Do ADO.NET Data Services and Web Services Differ?	184
What is Representational State Transfer (REST)?	184
Why Use ADO.NET Data Services?	185
Features at a Glance	185
Prerequisites	**186**
Exposing Data as a Service Using ADO.NET Data Services	**186**
Creating an ADO.NET Data Service	187
Using a Relational Database as the Data Source	189
Using Data Sources Other Than a Relational Database	192
Understanding the System.Services.Data Namespace	**194**
Restricting Access to Resources	**196**
Working with the ADO.NET Data Service Client Library	**197**
Generating the Client-Side Entity Classes	198

Inserting a Record	198
Updating a Record	199
Deleting a Record	200
Consuming an ADO.NET Data Service Using LINQ	201
Exposing a Stored Procedure as a URI	201
Handling Exceptions in ADO.NET Data Services	**202**
Batching ADO.NET Data Services Requests to Improve Performance	**204**
Debugging Your Data Service	204
References	**205**
Summary	**206**
Index	**207**

Preface

The ADO.NET Entity Framework, the next generation of Microsoft's data access technology, is an extended Object Relational Mapping (ORM) technology that makes it easy to tie together the data in your database with the objects in your applications. This is done by abstracting the object model of an application from its relational or logical model. It is an extended ORM in the sense that it provides many additional features over an ORM. Some of these features are:

- Entity Inheritance and Composition
- Identity Resolution and Change Tracking
- LINQ Support
- The Object Service Layer

This book is a clear and concise guide to the ADO.NET Entity Framework. Packed with plentiful code examples, this book helps you to learn the ADO.NET Entity Framework and ADO.NET Data Services and build a better data access layer for your application.

What This Book Covers

Chapter 1 is an introduction to the basics of the ADO.NET Entity Framework (EF), its usefulness, its features, and the benefits.

Chapter 2 discusses how you can get started with EF, create an Entity Data Model (EDM), and write a program to query data.

Chapter 3 gives a detailed explanation of entities, relationships, and each of the sections of the EDM.

Chapter 4 provides a sample application that illustrates how to perform CRUD operations against the EDM.

Chapter 5 discusses the Entity SQL query language and how to work with the Entity Client provider.

Chapter 6 includes a detailed discussion on LINQ to Entities with many code examples.

Chapter 7 provides a detailed discussion on the Object Services Layer and its helpful and useful features.

Chapter 8 provides an introduction to ADO.NET Data Services and how it can be used with the EDM to perform CRUD operations.

What You Need for This Book

To learn the concepts covered in this book, the reader should have a proper understanding and working knowledge of the following:

- ADO.NET
- ASP.NET
- C#

To execute the code samples in this book, the following technologies should be installed in your system:

- Visual Studio 2008
- Visual Studio 2008 SP1
- SQL Server 2005
- Windows XP/Vista/2003 or higher

Who This Book is For

This book is for C# developers who want an easier way to create their data access layer. You will need to be comfortable with ADO.NET, but you do not need to know anything about the Entity Framework. Along the way we will create some ASP.NET applications, so familiarity with this will be helpful.

Conventions

In this book, you will find various styles of text that help distinguish between different kinds of information. Let's look at some examples of these styles, and an explanation of their meaning.

Code words in text are shown as follows:

"We can include other contexts through the use of the `include` directive."

A block of code will be set as follows:

```
            <asp:BoundField DataField="FirstName" HeaderText="First
Name" SortExpression="FirstName" />
            <asp:BoundField DataField="LastName" HeaderText="Last
Name" SortExpression="LastName" />
```

When we wish to draw your attention to a particular part of a code block, the relevant lines or items will be made bold. Note that last two lines of the following code sample:

```
<FunctionImport Name="DeleteEmployee">
<Parameter Name="EmployeeID" Mode="In" Type="Int32" />
<Parameter Name="DepartmentID" Mode="In" Type="Int32" />
<Parameter Name="DesignationID" Mode="In" Type="Int32" />
```

Any command-line input and output will be written as follows:

edmgen /mode:fullgeneration /c:"Data Source=.;Initial Catalog=Payroll;User ID=sa;Password=joydip1@3;" /p:Payroll

New terms and **important words** are introduced in a bold-type font. Words that you see on the screen, in menus or dialog boxes for example, appear in our text like this: "clicking the **Next** button moves you to the next screen".

Important notes appear in a box like this with the Notes icon on the left..

Tips and tricks appear like this with the Tips icon on the left.

Reader Feedback

Feedback from our readers is always welcome. Let us know what you think about this book, what you liked or may have disliked. Reader feedback is important for us to develop titles that you really get the most out of.

To send us general feedback, simply drop an email to feedback@packtpub.com, making sure to mention the book title in the subject line of your message.

If there is a book that you need and would like to see us publish, please send us a note in the **SUGGEST A TITLE** form on www.packtpub.com or email suggest@packtpub.com.

If there is a topic that you have expertise in and you are interested in either writing or contributing to a book, see our author guide on www.packtpub.com/authors.

Customer Support

Now that you are the proud owner of a Packt book, we have a number of things to help you to get the most from your purchase.

Downloading the Example Code for the Book

Visit http://www.packtpub.com/files/code/5227_Code.zip to directly download the example code.

The downloadable files contain instructions on how to use them.

Errors

Although we have taken every care to ensure the accuracy of our contents, mistakes do happen. If you find a mistake in one of our books—maybe a mistake in text or code—we would be grateful if you would report this to us. By doing this you can save other readers from frustration, and help to improve subsequent versions of this book. If you find any errors, report them by visiting http://www.packtpub.com/support, selecting your book, clicking on the **let us know** link, and entering the details of your errors. Once your errors are verified, your submission will be accepted and the errata added to the list of existing errors. The existing errors can be viewed by selecting your title from http://www.packtpub.com/support.

Piracy

Piracy of copyright material on the Internet is an ongoing problem across all media. At Packt, we take the protection of our copyright and licenses very seriously. If you come across any illegal copies of our works in any form on the Internet, please provide the location address or website name immediately so we can pursue a remedy.

Please contact us at `copyright@packtpub.com` with a link to the suspected pirated material.

We appreciate your help in protecting our authors, and our ability to bring you valuable content.

Questions

You can contact us at `questions@packtpub.com` if you have a problem or question with some aspect of this book. We will do our best to address these questions and problems.

1
Introducing the ADO.NET Entity Framework

The **ADO.NET Entity Framework** is an extended Object Relational Mapping (ORM) technology from Microsoft that abstracts the object model of an application from its relational or logical model. That is, it isolates the object model from the way the data is actually represented in the relational store. This framework makes the conceptual model real by using an extended entity relationship model called the ADO.NET Entity Data Model.

This chapter gives you an introduction to the ADO.NET Entity Framework and also equips you with a brief understanding of the related terminologies. We will revisit each of the Entity Framework architectural components as we progress through this book. Our journey of the ADO.NET Entity Framework has just begun!

In this chapter, we will cover the following points:

- An overview of the ADO.NET Entity Framework
- The ADO.NET Entity Framework Architectural Components
- Features and benefits of the ADO.NET Entity Framework
- Installing the ADO.NET Entity Framework

But, before we delve deep into this amazing technology from Microsoft, let's take a quick look at the prerequisites for learning the concepts covered in this book.

What You should Know

To learn the concepts covered in this book, the reader should have a basic understanding of the following:

- Programming using ADO.NET
- C#
- Working with ASP.NET Web Applications
- SQL Server

Looking Back

Any application has two perspectives. They are the Data Model and the Object Model. While the Data Model defines the way the data is defined and stored, the Object Model defines how the same data will be represented to the user in the presentation layer or, is exposed to the other layers of the application. The Data Model of the application usually deals with the storage and retrieval of the application's data to and from the relational store.

The relational store is used for data persistence, consistency, concurrency, and security. It contains the application's data and typically comprises of a set of tables, views, functions, procedures, and the relationships. You typically use T-SQL to query against the relational store which returns result sets that contains columns and rows of data.

However, the data returned doesn't necessarily match with the application's object oriented programming model. Usually, we don't use the data returned in the same form in which it is returned from the relational store. We write the necessary code to transform the data returned from the relational store to business objects in the data access layer of the application. Similarly, you need into write code to transform your application's business objects into a form that can be persisted into your relational store. But, what if the schema of the underlying relational store changes?

To bridge this apparent mismatch between the data and the object models, ORM tools have evolved. They are used to reduce the code required to transform your application's business objects into a form that can be persisted into the relational store and vice-versa.

What is ADO.NET Entity Framework?

The ADO.NET Entity Framework is a type of ORM. It is a development platform that provides a layer of abstraction on top of the relational or logical model. In doing so, it isolates the object model of the application from the way the data is actually stored in the relational store. Developers can use the ADO.NET Entity Framework to program against an object model rather than the logical or relationship model.

This level of abstraction is achieved using the Entity Data Model (EDM)—an extended Entity Relationship Model. The EDM reduces the dependency of your domain object model on the database schema of the data store in use. We will discuss more on this topic later in this chapter.

Developers can use the ADO.NET Entity Framework to work with domain specific properties such as employee name employee address, contact details, etc, without having to be concerned with how the actual data is stored and represented in the underlying data store. The framework can take care of the necessary translations to either retrieve data from your data store, or, perform inserts, updates, and deletes.

Is It Just Another ORM?

The ADO.NET Entity Framework is an extended ORM technology from Microsoft. We say it is an extended ORM because it has many additional features compared to a typical ORM. ORMs often use metadata and factory classes to retrieve data or collections of data. On the contrary, using the Entity Framework, you can easily map your data to be accessible in a relational representation in the database to objects, no matter how the mapping is implemented. You can expose different data views to your application without having to change your relational schema. In essence, this allows the applications to have their own view of the data. The applications can even reuse the same views of data amongst themselves.

The major difference between the ADO.NET Entity Framework and ORM tools is in the Entity Data Model and the former's ability to query data using strongly typed LINQ. You can even use Entity SQL, a T-SQL like query language for querying the Entity Data Model, to execute dynamic queries. In addition to what a typical ORM framework provides, the ADO.NET Entity Framework provides and supports entity inheritance, entity composition, and a flexible, loosely coupled three tiered model consisting of the conceptual model, the mapping layer, and the storage model.

The ADO.NET Entity Framework enables you to even extend the existing schema. In other words, you can extend the generated entity classes to create your own custom entity classes. You can define relationships of any kind such as one-to-one, one-to-many, and even many-to-many. So, isn't it a better ORM?

The ADO.NET Entity Framework Architectural Components

The ADO.NET Entity Framework is comprised of the following components:

- The Entity Data Model
- LINQ to Entities
- Entity Client
- Entity SQL
- The Object Services Layer

The following figure illustrates the layers of the ADO.NET Entity Framework and how they are related to each other:

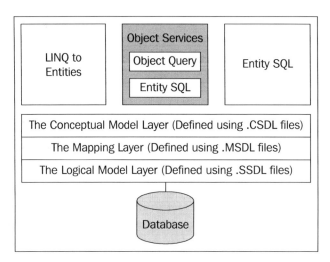

We will now discuss each of the components of the Entity Framework technology stack in the following sections.

The Entity Data Model (EDM)

The **Entity Data Model**, an extended entity relationship model, is the core of the ADO.NET Entity Framework.

You can generate an Entity Data Model using the EDMGen.exe command line tool, or, using the ADO.NET Entity Data Model designer—a new Visual Studio template. We will discuss how an Entity Data Model can be generated from a relational schema in the next chapter.

Chapter 1

The following figure illustrates where exactly the Entity Data Model fits in:

```
+---------------------------------------+
|   .NET Objects or collection of       |
|   .NET Objects                        |
+---------------------------------------+
|   The ADO.NET Entity Data Model       |
+---------------------------------------+
|   The Relational Data Store           |
+---------------------------------------+
```

The Entity Data Model abstracts the logical or the relational schema and exposes the conceptual schema of the data using a three-layered approach. It is comprised of the following layers:

- The Conceptual Data Definition Language Layer (C-Space)
- The Mapping Schema Definition Language Layer (C-S Space)
- The Store Space Definition Language Layer (S-Space)

The following figure illustrates the layers of the Entity Data Model:

```
+-------------------------------------------------------------------+
|              The ADO.NET Entity Data Model Layers                 |
+-------------------------------------------------------------------+
|              The Conceptual or the C-Space (GSDL)                 |
|                                                                   |
|  Comprises of EntityContainer, EntitySets, AssociationSets,       |
|  Association Types, EntityTypes, Relationships and Functions      |
|                                                                   |
|  Queried using Entity SQL or ESQL (EntityConnection,              |
|  EntityCommand, EntityDataReader)                                 |
+-------------------------------------------------------------------+
|                                                                   |
|         The Mapping Layer or the C-S Mapping Layer (MSL)          |
|                                                                   |
+-------------------------------------------------------------------+
|               The Logical or the S-Space (SSDL)                   |
|                                                                   |
|  Comprises of Tables, Stored Procedures, Views and Functions      |
|                                                                   |
|             Queried using ADO.NET Data Providers                  |
|  (SQLConnection, SQLCommand, SQLDataReader, SQLDataAdapter,       |
|           etc using T-SQL or, using PL-SQL)                       |
+-------------------------------------------------------------------+
```

The **Conceptual Layer or the C-Space Layer** is responsible for defining the entities and their relationships. It defines your business objects and their relationships in XML files. The C-Space is modeled using CSDL and is comprised of EntityContainer, EntitySets, AssociationSets, AssociationTypes, EntityTypes, and Functions. You can query this layer using Entity SQL or ESQL (EntityConnection, EntityCommand, and EntityDataReader).

The **C-S Mapping Layer** is responsible for mapping the conceptual and the logical layers. That is, it maps the business objects and the relationships defined in the conceptual layer with the tables and relationships defined in the logical layer. It is a mapping system created in XML, which links or maps the Conceptual and the Logical layers. The C-S Mapping layer is modeled using MSL.

The **Logical or the Storage Layer** (also called the S-Space) represents the schema of the underlying database. This is comprised of tables, stored procedures, view, and functions. It is modeled using SSDL and queried using ADO.NET Data Providers. Hence, we use SQLConnection, SQLCommand, SQLDataReader, and SQLDataAdapter using T-SQL or PL-SQL if our data store is a SQL database.

Here is how a typical Entity Data Model looks:

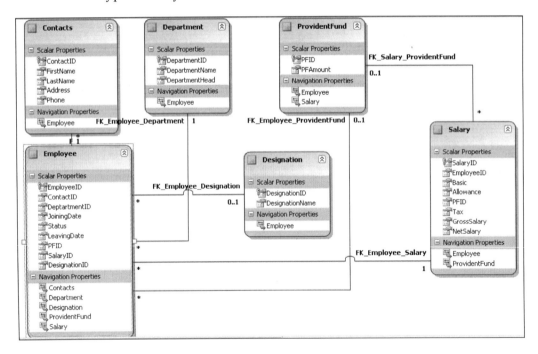

Chapter 1

How is the Entity Data Model Represented?

The Entity Data Model uses the following three types of XML files to represent the C-Space, C-S Space, and the S-Space respectively.

- .CSDL (Conceptual Schema Definition Language): This represents the C-S Space and is used to map the entity types used in the conceptual model.
- .MSL (Mapping Schema Language): This represents the C-S Space and is used to map the logical model to the conceptual model.
- .SSDL (Store Schema Definition Language): This represents the S-Space and is used to map the schema information of the logical layer.

> If you use the ADO.NET Entity Data Model Designer tool to generate your Entity Data Model, you will have one .edmx file that contains the CSDL, MSL, and SSDL sections bundled into one single file. At runtime, the .csdl, .msl, and .ssdl files are created in the application's output directory.

These files store the metadata information as XML for each of the above layers. Here is what the CSDL section of your Entity Data Model looks like:

```
<!-- CSDL content -->
<edmx:ConceptualModels>
<EntityContainer Name="PayrollEntities">
        <EntitySet Name="Designation" EntityType="PayrollModel.Designation" />
      </EntityContainer>
      <EntityType Name="Designation">
        <Key>
          <PropertyRef Name="DesignationID" />
        </Key>
        <Property Name="DesignationID" Type="Int32" Nullable="false" />
        <Property Name="DesignationName" Type="String" Nullable="false" MaxLength="50" Unicode="false" />
        <NavigationProperty Name="Employee" Relationship="PayrollModel.FK_Employee_Designation" FromRole="Designation" ToRole="Employee" />
      </EntityType>
</edmx:ConceptualModels>
```

Introducing the ADO.NET Entity Framework

Here is how a typical SSDL section of the Entity Data Model looks like:

```xml
<!-- SSDL content -->
    <edmx:StorageModels>
        <EntityContainer Name="dbo">
            <EntitySet Name="Designation" EntityType=
"PayrollModel.Store.Designation" />
        </EntityContainer>
        <EntityType Name="Designation">
          <Key>
            <PropertyRef Name="DesignationID" />
          </Key>
          <Property Name="DesignationID" Type="int" Nullable="false"
StoreGeneratedPattern="Identity" />
          <Property Name="DesignationName" Type="varchar"
Nullable="false" MaxLength="50" />
        </EntityType>
      </Schema>
    </edmx:StorageModels>
```

And here is the C-S maping section for you:

```xml
<!-- C-S mapping content -->
    <edmx:Mappings>
        <Mapping Space="C-S" xmlns="urn:schemas-microsoft-com:windows:
storage:mapping:CS">
          <EntityContainerMapping StorageEntityContainer="dbo"
CdmEntityContainer="PayrollEntities">
            <EntitySetMapping Name="Designation">
              <EntityTypeMapping TypeName="IsTypeOf(PayrollModel.
Designation)">
                <MappingFragment StoreEntitySet="Designation">
                  <ScalarProperty Name="DesignationID" ColumnName=
"DesignationID" />
                  <ScalarProperty Name="DesignationName" ColumnName=
"DesignationName" />
                </MappingFragment>
              </EntityTypeMapping>
            </EntitySetMapping>
          </EntityContainerMapping>
        </Mapping>
      </edmx:Mappings>
   </edmx:Runtime>
</edmx:Edmx>
```

> You can also create abstract and complex types in your Entity Data Model. You can derive from an abstract type to create sub-types, but no instance of the abstract type can be created. You can also create complex types. That is, types that don't have any identity of their own. A typical example of a complex type is the Address type.

We will skip further discussion on each of the sections of an Entity Data Model until Chapter 3.

The Object Model (O-Space)

When working with the **ADO.NET Entity Framework**, you will have an **Object Model** on top of all the **Entity Data Model** layers. You need to model the Object Model using .NET objects. The following figure illustrates how the Object Model fits in with the EDM layers:

```
+-------------------------------------------------------+
|           The Object Model or the O-Space            |
+-------------------------------------------------------+
|                The O-C Mapping Layer                  |
+-------------------------------------------------------+
| The Conceptual Model or the C-Space (Modelled using CSDL) |
+-------------------------------------------------------+
| The Mapping Layer or the C-S Space (Modelled using MSL)   |
+-------------------------------------------------------+
| The Logical Model or the S-Space (Modelled using SSDL)    |
+-------------------------------------------------------+
```

The Object Model Layer contains, .NET objects, collection of .NET objects, types, properties and methods. You can use the Object Model or the O-Space Model to query your business objects, or the collections of your business objects, using LINQ to Entities or Entity SQL. The C-Space and O-Space models are actually mapped by the O-C Mapping Layer using code attributes applied to the O-space Model.

LINQ to Entities

Language Integrated Query (LINQ) is a query translation pipeline that has been introduced as part of the C# 3.0 library. It comprises a set of query operators for different data sources (LDAP, Objects, CSV, XML, Entities, SQL, etc.). It is an extension of the C# language and provides a simplified framework for accessing relational data in a strongly typed, Object Oriented manner.

LINQ to Entities is a Microsoft technology that enables you to query your business objects from within the language in a strongly typed manner. You can use LINQ to Entities, a superset of LINQ to SQL, to query data against a conceptual data model, namely, the Entity Data Model. We will learn more on LINQ and LINQ to Entities in the chapter 6.

Here is an example of a typical LINQ to Entities query:

```
PayrollModel.PayrollEntities ctx = new PayrollModel.PayrollEntities();
    var query = from emp in ctx.Employee
        select emp;
    foreach (var employee in query)
        Response.Write("<BR>"+employee.FirstName);
```

> LINQ to Entities rests on top of the ADO.NET Entity Framework's Object Services Layer and that the LINQ to Entities queries are internally translated to canonical query trees. This, in turn, gets converted internally to corresponding SQL queries in a form expected by your underlying database.

Entity Client

Entity Client, the gateway to entity-level queries, is the Entity Framework's counterpart of ADO.NET's SQL Client or Oracle Client that uses Entity SQL or E-SQL to query the conceptual model. You create a connection using Entity Connection, execute commands through Entity Commands, and retrieve the result sets as Entity Data Readers.

Entity SQL

Entity SQL is a data store independent derivative of T-SQL that supports entity inheritance and relationships. You can use it to query data using the conceptual schema. You can even build your own dynamic queries. These E-SQL queries are internally translated to data store dependent SQL queries. This translation, that is, the conversion of the E-SQL queries to their data store-specific query language like T-SQL, (it doesn't need to be only T-SQL, however, it is the supported one) is handled by the Entity Framework. Entity SQL or E-SQL may not be as strongly typed as LINQ is, but, you have the flexibility of executing dynamic queries using it, much like T-SQL.

Strongly typed data access is one of the most striking features of LINQ. LINQ queries are checked at compile time. This is unlike SQL queries which are only detected at runtime.

But, why do you need Entity SQL when you have LINQ to Entities to query data through you Entity Data Model? You can, using Entity SQL, compose queries that are difficult to determine until the time the query is executed. On a different note, Entity SQL is a full text-based query language that you can use in much the same way as you use ADO.NET data providers.

Here is an example that shows how you can use Entity SQL to insert data in your applications.

```
using (EntityConnection conn = new EntityConnection("Name=PayrollEnti
ties"))
    {
        try
        {
            conn.Open();
            EntityCommand cmd = conn.CreateCommand();
            cmd.CommandText = "PayrollEntities.AddNewEmployee";
            cmd.CommandType = CommandType.StoredProcedure;
            cmd.Parameters.AddWithValue("FirstName", "Joydip");
            cmd.Parameters.AddWithValue("LastName", "Kanjilal");
            cmd.Parameters.AddWithValue("Address", "Hyderabad");
            cmd.Parameters.AddWithValue("DepartmentID", 4);
            cmd.ExecuteNonQuery();
        }
        catch (Exception ex)
        {
            Response.Write(ex.ToString());
        }
    }
```

 To query data from the Entity Data Model, you have three choices—Entity SQL, LINQ to Entities, and Object Services.

Avoiding Complex Joins

You can use Entity SQL to avoid complex joins as you will typically be querying against a conceptual model of the data. As an example, if we want to display employee names and the department names in which they work, we would have to join the information of the Employee and the Department tables and then filter the unwanted columns to retrieve only the information that is required. Such traversals become a nightmare as you add additional tables and you therefore require more complex joins.

When you implement your Object Model using Object Oriented Programming Languages, you expose the object's relationships with other objects of its kind using properties. This is in contrast to the approach we just discussed. Hence, designing an Object Model using this approach is cumbersome. This is exactly where the ADO.NET Entity Framework fits in; it represents the conceptual and logical model of data while using grammar that is common to both.

Here is a code snippet that explains how you can use Entity SQL to avoid complex joins in your application's code. The following T-SQL query can be used to retrieve employee data split across three tables, namely, Employee, Department, and Salary.

```
Select Employee.FirstName, Employee.LastName, Department.
DepartmentName, Salary.Basic
from Employee
INNER JOIN
Department on Department.DepartmentID = Employee.DepartmentID
INNER JOIN
Salary on Salary.EmployeeID = Employee.EmployeeID
```

And, here is how you will use the Entity SQL to achieve the same result:

```
Select FirstName, LastName, DepartmentName, Basic from EmployeeData
```

The Object Services Layer

Apart from querying the Conceptual Model, you might, at some point, have to work with entities such as in-memory objects or a collection of in-memory objects. To do this you need Object Services. You can use it to query data, from almost any data store, with less code. In addition to from enabling you to perform CRUD operations, the Object Services Layer provides the following additional services:

- Change tracking
- Lazy loading
- Inheritance
- Optimistic concurrency
- Merging data
- Identity resolution
- Support for querying data using Entity SQL and LINQ to Entities

We will learn more about Object Services later in the book. The Object Services Layer internally uses an Object Query object for query processing. Note that the Object Services Layer supports querying data using both Entity SQL and LINQ to Entities.

> You can query data from the Entity Data Model either using Object Services or Entity Client. However, if you require change tracking, be aware that only Object Services provides this feature. Note that in either case, the ADO.NET Data Providers are responsible for talking to the underlying database.

Here is an example that shows how you can use Object Services to retrieve data.

```
using (ObjectContext ctx = new ObjectContext("Name=PayrollEntities"))
    {
        var query = from employee in ctx.CreateQuery<PayrollModel.Employee>("PayrollEntities.Employee") select employee;
        foreach (PayrollModel.Employee emp in query)
        {
            Response.Write("<BR>" + emp.FirstName);
        }
    }
```

ADO.NET Entity Framework—Features and Benefits at a Glance

Here is a quick look at some of the features and benefits of the ADO.NET Entity Framework:

- Increased level of abstraction.
- An extensible and flexible provider model.
- Seamless querying of data using Entity SQL and LINQ.
- A flexible schema for storing the mapping information.
- Reduction to the amount of KLOC needed to write data access code in your applications.
- Provides a layer of abstraction on top of any data store as long as an implementation for the underlying data store is provided.
- A powerful Object Services Layer.
- A full text-based query language.
- Support for a conceptual data model of an application.

Introducing the ADO.NET Entity Framework

 KLOC refers to Kilo Lines of Code, a unit of measuring the amount of source code in your programs.

Installing the Prerequisites

To run the programs given in this book, you should have the following elements installed on your system:

- Visual Studio.NET 2008 Professional
- SQL Server 2005 or higher
- Microsoft .NET Framework 3.5 SP1
- ADO.NET Entity Framework Beta 3 or higher
- ADO.NET Entity Framework Tools December 2007 CTP or higher

Installing the ADO.NET Entity Framework and Its Tools

Before you proceed with installing EF Beta 3 and its tools, make sure that you have installed Visual Studio.NET 2008 Professional and SQL Server 2005 on your system. I will skip the discussion on installing Visual Studio 2008 Professional and SQL Server 2005 at this time.

Downloading the Software

Let us take a look at the necessary software that you need to download in order to work with the ADO.NET Entity Framework.

- Download ADO.NET Entity Framework Beta 3 from the following link:

  http://www.microsoft.com/downloads/details.aspx?FamilyId=15DB9989-1621-444D-9B18-D1A04A21B519&displaylang=en

- Download ADO.NET Entity Framework Tools December 2007 CTP from the link give below:

  http://www.microsoft.com/downloads/details.aspx?FamilyId=D8AE4404-8E05-41FC-94C8-C73D9E238F82&displaylang=en

- Download the patch update to Visual Studio.NET 2008 from the link given below:

  http://go.microsoft.com/fwlink/?LinkID=104985

- Download Microsoft .NET Framework 3.5 SP1 from the following link:

  http://www.microsoft.com/downloads/details.aspx?FamilyId=8C36ACA4-E947-4760-9B05-93CAC04C6F87&displaylang=en

Installing the Software

Now that the required software has been downloaded, we will now install each one individually.

Double-click on the ADO.NET Entity Framework Setup file. The following installation wizard window will appear:

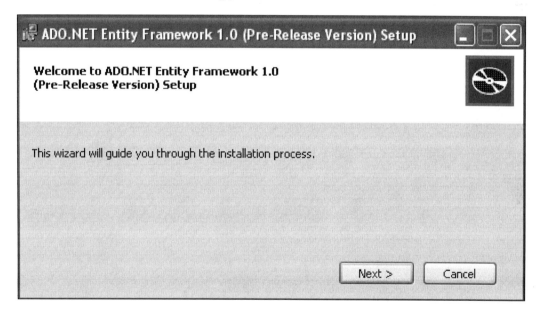

Now, click on **Next**.

Introducing the ADO.NET Entity Framework

Here is how the next screen looks like:

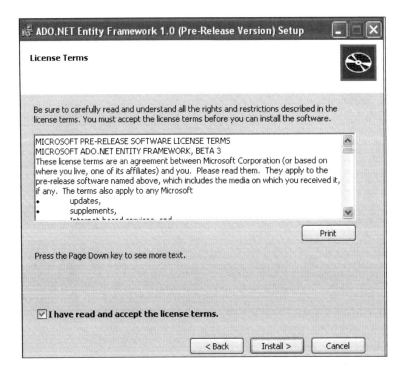

In the above window that appears, check the checkbox and click on **Install**.

The installation procedure starts and when done, the following screen appears:

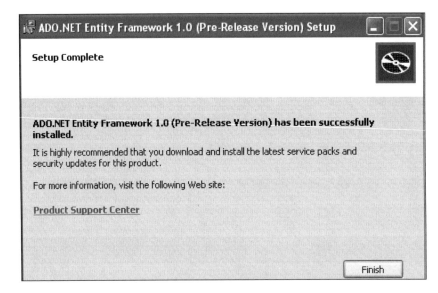

Click on **Finish** to complete the installation process.

Now that you have installed the ADO.NET Entity Framework successfully on your system, the next step is to install the ADO.NET Entity Framework Tools CTP. But before you do that, you need to install the Visual Studio.NET 2008 patch update.

Double-click on the Visual Studio.NET patch update setup file that you downloaded earlier. The following window appears:

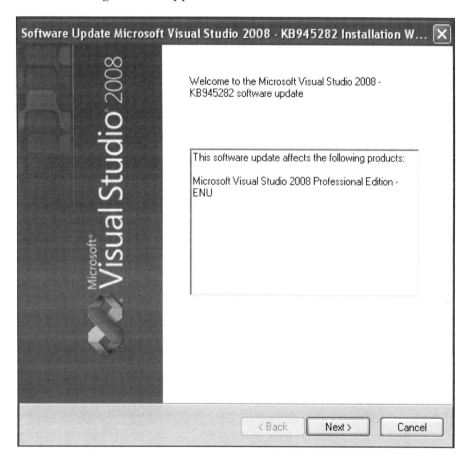

Now, click on **Next**.

The following window appears:

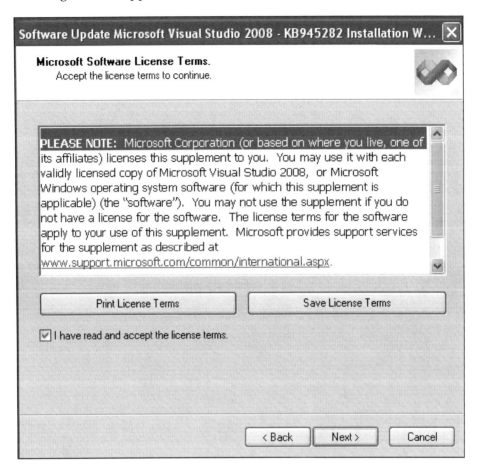

Check the check box to agree and accept the license terms and click on **Next** to start the installation process.

Once the installation is complete, the following window appears:

Chapter 1

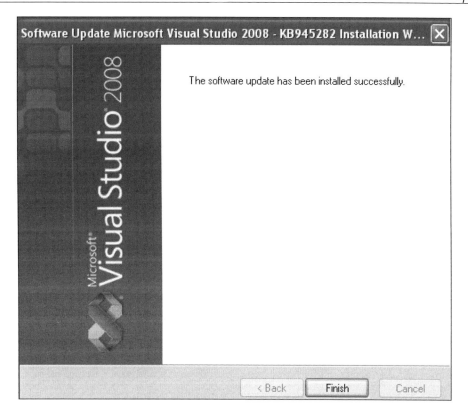

Click on **Finish** to complete the installation process.

Now, we need to install the ADO.NET Entity Framework Tools CTP. To do this, double-click on the ADO.NET Entity Framework December 2007 Tools CTP you downloaded earlier. The following screen appears:

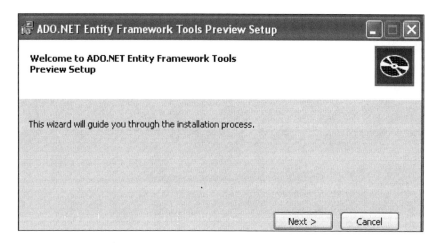

Click on **Next**. The following window appears:

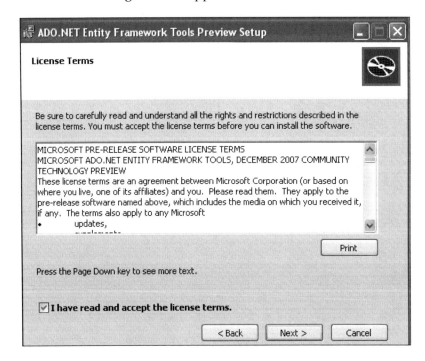

Now, check the check box to accept the license terms and click on **Next**. The following window will appear:

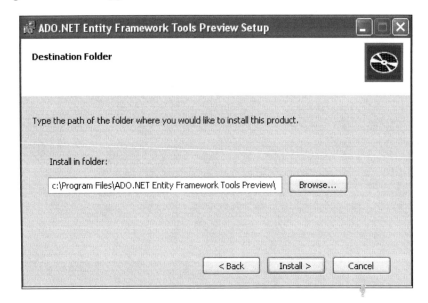

Click on **Install** to start the installation process. Once the installation is complete, the following window is displayed:

Clink on **Finish** to complete the installation process.

We will now install Microsoft .NET Framework 3.5 SP1. It contains many additional features and most importantly, we need it to work with the Entity Data Source control. We will discuss this control in the next chapter.

Introducing the ADO.NET Entity Framework

To install Microsoft .NET Framework 3.5 SP1 on your system, double-click on the setup file you downloaded earlier. The following screenshot shows the window that will appear:

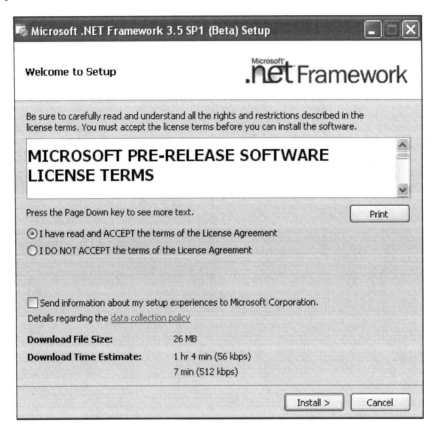

Select the radio button to accept the terms of the license agreement and click on **Install** to start the installation process.

Once the installation process is complete, the following window is displayed:

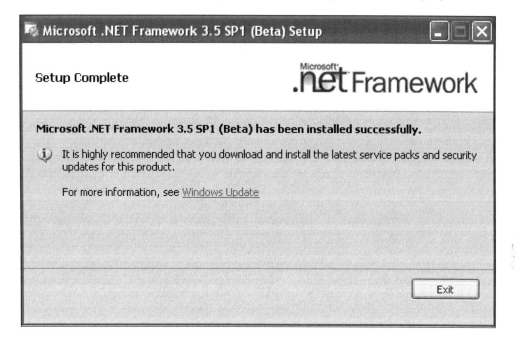

Click on **Exit** to complete the installation process. You are done!

Having installed these prerequisites, we will now design our sample database. We will use this database throughout this book. We will assign the name Payroll to our design database. The next section discusses the design of this sample database.

Designing the Payroll Database

In this section, we will design our Payroll database, which we will use throughout this book. This database will comprised of the following five tables:

- Employee
- Department
- Designation
- Salary
- Provident Fund

Introducing the ADO.NET Entity Framework

Here is the script for creating these tables.

```
CREATE TABLE [dbo].[Employee](
    [EmployeeID] [int] IDENTITY(1,1) NOT NULL,
    [FirstName] [varchar](50) COLLATE SQL_Latin1_General_CP1_CI_AS NOT NULL,
    [LastName] [varchar](50) COLLATE SQL_Latin1_General_CP1_CI_AS NOT NULL,
    [Address] [varchar](50) COLLATE SQL_Latin1_General_CP1_CI_AS NOT NULL,
    [Phone] [varchar](50) COLLATE SQL_Latin1_General_CP1_CI_AS NOT NULL,
    [DepartmentID] [int] NOT NULL,
    [JoiningDate] [datetime] NOT NULL,
    [LeavingDate] [datetime] NULL,
    [DesignationID] [int] NOT NULL,
 CONSTRAINT [PK_Employee] PRIMARY KEY CLUSTERED
(
    [EmployeeID] ASC
)WITH (IGNORE_DUP_KEY = OFF) ON [PRIMARY]
) ON [PRIMARY]
CREATE TABLE [dbo].[Department](
    [DepartmentID] [bigint] NOT NULL,
    [DepartmentName] [varchar](50) COLLATE SQL_Latin1_General_CP1_CI_AS NOT NULL,
    [DepartmentHead] [bigint] NOT NULL,
 CONSTRAINT [PK_Department] PRIMARY KEY CLUSTERED
(
    [DepartmentID] ASC
)WITH (IGNORE_DUP_KEY = OFF) ON [PRIMARY]
) ON [PRIMARY]
CREATE TABLE [dbo].[Designation](
    [DesignationID] [bigint] NOT NULL,
    [DesignationName] [varchar](50) COLLATE SQL_Latin1_General_CP1_CI_AS NOT NULL,
 CONSTRAINT [PK_Designation] PRIMARY KEY CLUSTERED
(
    [DesignationID] ASC
)WITH (IGNORE_DUP_KEY = OFF) ON [PRIMARY]
) ON [PRIMARY]
CREATE TABLE [dbo].[Salary](
    [SalaryID] [bigint] NOT NULL,
    [EmployeeID] [bigint] NOT NULL,
    [Basic] [money] NOT NULL,
    [Allowance] [money] NOT NULL,
    [PFID] [bigint] NULL,
    [Tax] [money] NOT NULL,
    [GrossSalary] [money] NOT NULL,
```

```
    [NetSalary] [money] NOT NULL,
 CONSTRAINT [PK_Salary] PRIMARY KEY CLUSTERED
(
    [SalaryID] ASC
)WITH (IGNORE_DUP_KEY = OFF) ON [PRIMARY]
) ON [PRIMARY]
CREATE TABLE [dbo].[ProvidentFund](
    [PFID] [bigint] NOT NULL,
    [PFAmount] [money] NOT NULL,
 CONSTRAINT [PK_ProvidentFund] PRIMARY KEY CLUSTERED
(
    [PFID] ASC
)WITH (IGNORE_DUP_KEY = OFF) ON [PRIMARY]
) ON [PRIMARY]
```

Here is how the database diagram for our Payroll database looks:

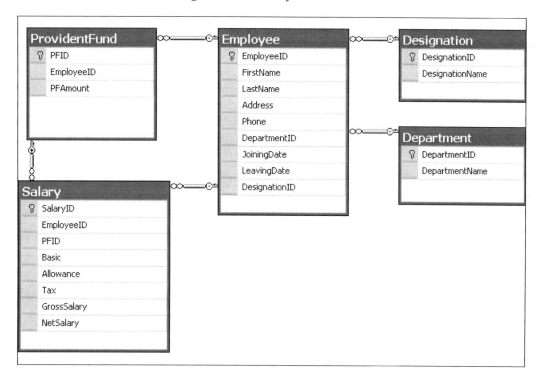

Introducing the ADO.NET Entity Framework

We will create some stored procedures now that we will use to insert, update, and delete data from the tables we just created. Here is a list of the stored procedures that we will create for our Payroll database:

- Employee_Insert
- Employee_Update
- Employee_Delete
- Department_Insert
- Department_Update
- Department_Delete
- Designation_Insert
- Designation_Update
- Designation_Delete
- ProvidentFund_Insert
- ProvidentFund_Update
- ProvidentFund_Delete
- Salary_Insert
- Salary_Update
- Salary_Delete

Here is the script for these procedures.

```
Create Procedure Employee_Insert
As
@FirstName varchar(50), @LastName varchar(50), @Address varchar(50),
@Phone varchar(50), @DepartmentID int, @DesignationID int,
@JoiningDate datetime, @LeavingDate datetime
as
Insert into Employee(DepartmentID, DesignationID, JoiningDate,
LeavingDate) values (@DepartmentID, @DesignationID, @JoiningDate,
@LeavingDate)
Go
Create Procedure Employee_Update
@EmployeeID int, @FirstName varchar(50), @LastName varchar(50),
@Address varchar(50), @Phone varchar(50), @DepartmentID int,
@DesignationID int
as
Update Employee Set DepartmentID = @DepartmentID, DesignationID =
@DesignationID Where Employee.EmployeeID = @EmployeeID
```

```sql
Go
Create Procedure Employee_Delete
@EmployeeID int
as
Delete from Employee where Employee.EmployeeID = @EmployeeID
Go
Create Procedure Department_Insert
@DepartmentName varchar(50)
as
Insert into Department (DepartmentName) values (@DepartmentName)
Go
Create Procedure Department_Update
@DepartmentID int,@DepartmentName varchar(50)
as
Update Department Set DepartmentName = @DepartmentName where
DepartmentID = @DepartmentID
Go
Create Procedure Department_Delete
@DepartmentID int
as
Delete from Department where DepartmentID = @DepartmentID
Go
Create Procedure Designation_Insert
@DesignationName varchar(50)
as
Insert into Designation (DesignationName) values (@DesignationName)
Go
Create Procedure Designation_Update
@DesignationID int, @DesignationName varchar(50)
as
Update Designation Set DesignationName = @DesignationName where
DesignationID=@DesignationID
Go
Create Procedure Designation_Delete
@DesignationID int
as
Delete from Designation where DesignationID=@DesignationID
Go
Create Procedure ProvidentFund_Insert
@EmployeeID int, @PFAmount money
as
Insert into ProvidentFund (EmployeeID, PFAmount) values (@EmployeeID,
@PFAmount)
```

```
Go
Create Procedure ProvidentFund_Update
@PFID int, @EmployeeID int, @PFAmount money
as
Update ProvidentFund set EmployeeID = @EmployeeID, PFAmount =
@PFAmount where PFID = @PFID
Go
Create Procedure ProvidentFund_Delete
@PFID int
as
Delete from ProvidentFund where PFID = @PFID
Go
Create Procedure Salary_Insert
@EmployeeID int, @PFID int, @Basic money, @Allowance money,
@Tax money, @GrossSalary money, @NetSalary money
as
Insert into Salary(EmployeeID, PFID, Basic, Allowance, Tax,
GrossSalary, NetSalary) values (@EmployeeID, @PFID, @Basic,
@Allowance, @Tax, @GrossSalary, @NetSalary)
Go
Create Procedure Salary_Update
@SalaryID int, @EmployeeID int, @PFID int, @Basic money, @Allowance
money, @Tax money, @GrossSalary money, @NetSalary money
as
Update Salary set EmployeeID = @EmployeeID, PFID = @PFID, Basic =
@Basic, Allowance = @Allowance, Tax = @Tax, GrossSalary = @
GrossSalary, NetSalary = @NetSalary where SalaryID = @SalaryID
Go
Create Procedure Salary_Delete
@SalaryID int
as
Delete from Salary where SalaryID = @SalaryID
```

We will add more tables and stored procedures to our Payroll database as necessary in the chapters to follow.

Summary

The ADO.NET Entity Framework mainly addressees how easily you can persist and query your data with many of added services. You can use the ADO.NET Entity Framework to focus on the object model rather than the logical model. In other words, you can add a level of abstraction on top of your relational store.

In this chapter, we have had a look at what this framework is, its architecture, advantages, and how it differs from LINQ to SQL (formerly called DLINQ). In the next chapter, we will learn how to get started with the ADO.NET Entity Framework.

Glossary

Entity: This is the core concept in the Entity Framework. An Entity essentially models individual objects, like, employees, customers, etc. It is something that is uniquely definable, distinctly identifiable, and contains information pertaining to the entity.

Relational or Logical Model: A relational or logical model depicts the logical view of data that comprises of the normalized entities and their inter-relationships in a database.

Object Model: An Object Model may be defined as a collection of the objects, members, and properties of a class and the relationships between them that illustrates the structure of a system. An Object Model of a system is centered on the three basic properties of Object Oriented Programming—encapsulation, abstraction, and inheritance.

The **Entity Data Model (EDM)** is an implementation for the Entity – Relationship model (commonly called the E-R model). It depicts the entities and their relationships. The EDM is a view of the data store that your application will use.

2
Getting Started

In the previous chapter we took a look at the ADO.NET Entity Framework including its architecture and its features. We also designed our Payroll database that we will be using throughout this book to store and retrieve data. We will use the same database in this chapter to generate an Entity Data Model and then use it, along with the Entity Data Source control, to bind data to a GridView data control.

In this chapter, we will cover the following points:

- Creating an Entity Data Model
- Introducing the Entity Data Source Control
- Implementing our first application using the ADO.NET Entity Framework

We will start this chapter with a discussion on how we can create an Entity Data Model from our Payroll database.

Creating an Entity Data Model

You can create the ADO.NET Entity Data Model in one of two ways:

- Use the ADO.NET Entity Data Model Designer
- Use the command line Entity Data Model Designer called EdmGen.exe

We will first take a look at how we can design an Entity Data Model using the ADO.NET Entity Data Model Designer which is a Visual Studio wizard that is enabled after you install ADO.NET Entity Framework and its tools. It provides a graphical interface that you can use to generate an Entity Data Model.

Getting Started

Creating the Payroll Entity Data Model Using the ADO.NET Entity Data Model Designer

Here again are the tables of our Payroll database that we will use to generate the data model:

- Employee
- Designation
- Department
- Salary
- ProvidentFund

To create an entity data model using the ADO.NET Entity Data Model Designer, follow these simple steps:

1. Open Visual Studio.NET and create a solution for a new web application project as seen below and save with a name.

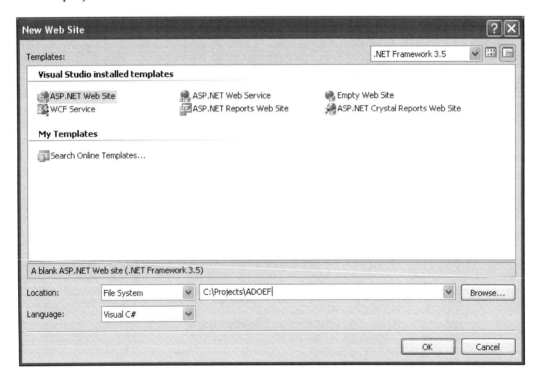

2. Switch to the Solution Explorer, right click and click on **Add New Item** as seen in the following screenshot:

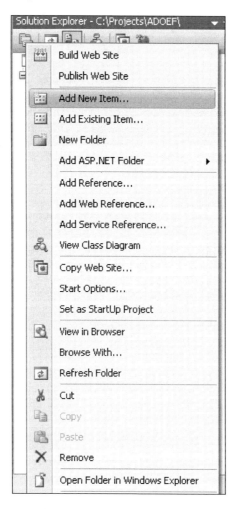

Getting Started

3. Next, select **ADO.NET Entity Data Model** from the list of the templates displayed as shown in the following screenshot:

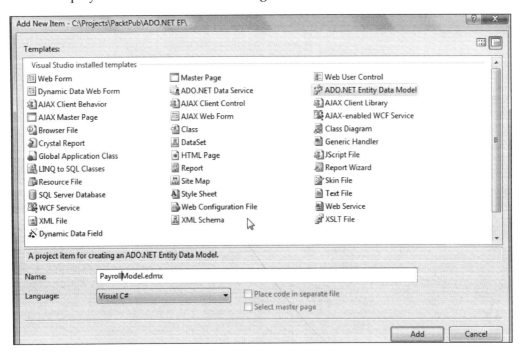

4. Name the Entity Data Model **PayrollModel** and click on **Add.**
5. Select **Generate from database** from the Entity Data Model Wizard as shown in the following screenshot:

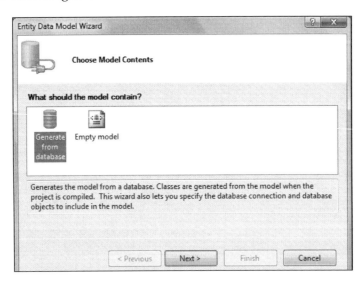

Chapter 2

Note that you can also use the Empty model template to create the Entity Data Model yourself.

If you select the Empty Data Model template and click on next, the following screen appears:

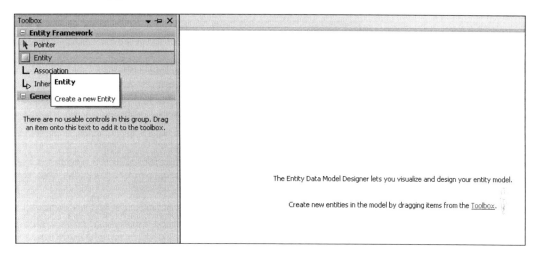

As you can see from the above figure, you can use this template to create the Entity Data Model yourself. You can create the Entity Types and their relationships manually by dragging items from the toolbox. We will not use this template in our discussion here. So, let's get to the next step.

6. Click on **Next** in the Entity Data Model Wizard window shown earlier.

Getting Started

7. The modal dialog box will now appear and prompts you to choose your connection as shown in the following figure:

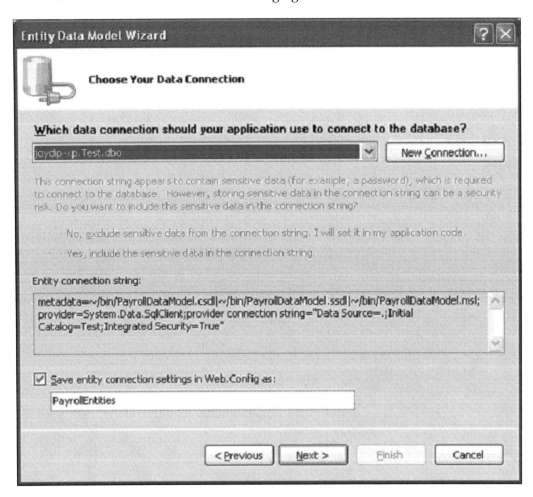

8. Click on **New Connection** Now you will need to specify the connection properties and parameters as shown in the following figure:

Chapter 2

 We will use a dot to specify the database server name. This implies that we will be using the database server of the localhost, which is the current system in use.

9. After you specify the necessary user name, password, and the server name, you can test your connection using the **Test Connection** button. When you do so, the message **Test connection succeeded** gets displayed in the message box as shown in the previous figure.

Getting Started

10. When you click on **OK on the Test connection dialog box,** the following screen appears:

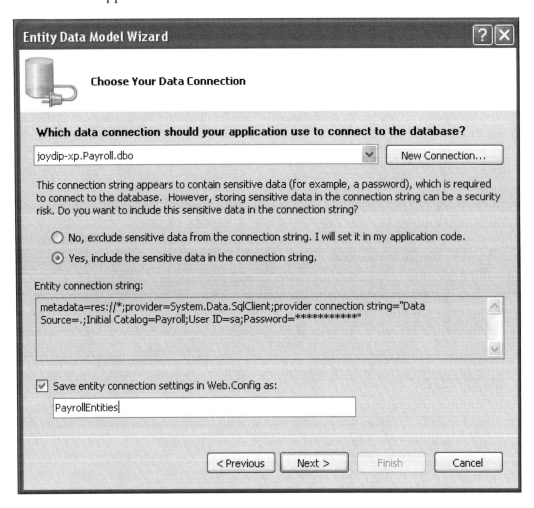

Note the Entity Connection String generated automatically. This connection string will be saved in the ConnectionStrings section of your application's web.config file. This is how it will look like:

```
<connectionStrings>
  <add name="PayrollEntities" connectionString="metadata=res://
    *;provider=System.Data.SqlClient;provider connection
    string=&quot;Data Source=.;Initial Catalog=Payroll;User
    ID=sa;Password=joydip1@3;MultipleActiveResultSets=True&quot;"
    providerName="System.Data.EntityClient" />
</connectionStrings>
```

11. When you click on **Next** in the previous figure, the following screen appears:

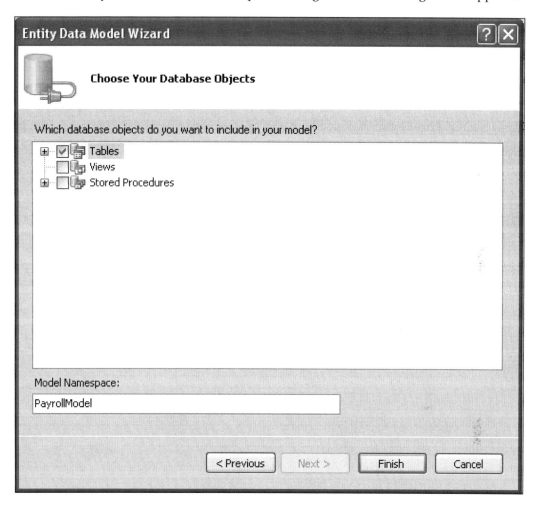

Getting Started

12. Expand the **Tables** node and specify the database objects that you require in the Entity Data Model to be generated as shown in the following figure:

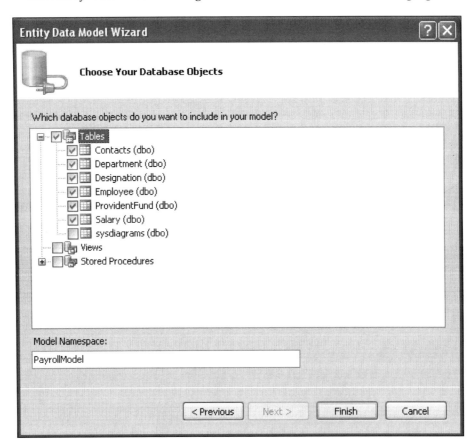

13. Click on **Finish** to generate the Entity Data Model.

Here is the output displayed in the Output Window while the Entity Data Model is being generated:

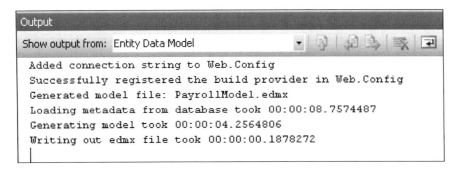

Chapter 2

Your Entity Data Model has been generated and saved in a file named `PayrollModel.edmx`. We are done creating our first Entity Data Model using the ADO.NET Entity Data Model Designer tool.

When you open the Payroll Entity Data Model that we just created in the designer view, it will appear as shown in the following figure:

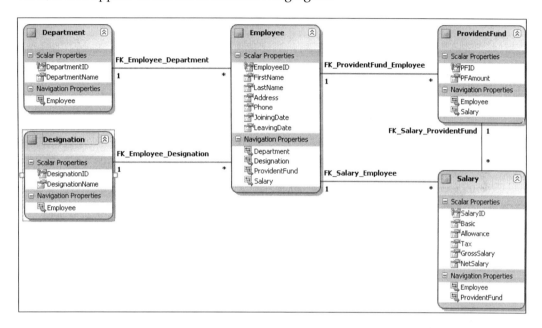

Note how the Entity Types in the above model are related to one another. These relationships have been generated automatically by the Entity Data Model Designer based on the relationships between the tables of the Payroll database we created in the previous chapter.

In the next section, we will learn how we can create an Entity Data Model using the EdmGen.exe command line tool.

Creating the Payroll Data Model Using the EdmGen Tool

We will now take a look at how to create a data model using the Entity Data Model generation tool called **EdmGen**.

Getting Started

The EdmGen.exe command line tool can be used to do one or more of the following:

- Generate the .cdsl, .msl, and .ssdl files as part of the Entity Data Model
- Generate object classes from a .csdl file
- Validate an Entity Data Model

The EdmGen.exe command line tool generates the Entity Data Model as a set of three files: .csdl, .msl, and .ssdl. If you have used the ADO.NET Entity Data Model Designer to generate your Entity Data Model, the .edmx file generated will contain the CSDL, MSL, and the SSDL sections. You will have a single .edmx file that bundles all of these sections into it. On the other hand, if you use the EdmGen.exe tool to generate the Entity Data Model, you would find three distinctly separate files with .csdl, .msl or .ssdl extensions.

Here is a list of the major options of the EdmGen.exe command line tool:

Option	Description
/help	Use this option to display help on all the possible options of this tool. The short form is /?
/language:CSharp	Use this option to generate code using C# language
/language:VB	Use this option to generate code using VB language
/provider:<string>	Use this option to specify the name of the ADO.NET data provider that you would like to use.
/connectionstring: <connection string>	Use this option to specify the connection string to be used to connect to the database
/namespace:<string>	Use this option to specify the name of the namespace
/mode:FullGeneration	Use this option to generate your CSDL, MSL, and SSDL objects from the database schema
/mode:EntityClassGeneration	Use this option to generate your entity classes from a given CSDL file
/mode:FromSsdlGeneration	Use this option to generate MSL, CSDL, and Entity Classes from a given SSDL file
/mode:ValidateArtifacts	Use this option to validate the CSDL, SSDL, and MSL files
/mode:ViewGeneration	Use this option to generate mapping views from the CSDL, SSDL, and MSL files

Option	Description
/entitycontainer:<string>	Use this option to specify the name of the Entity Container to be used in the conceptual model
/project:<string>	Use this option to specify the base name to be used for all the artifact files (.csdl, .msl, .ssdl) to be generated. The short form of this option is /p

Note that you basically need to pass the connection string, specify the mode, and also the project name of the artifact files (.csdl, .msl, and the .ssdl files) to be created. To create the Entity Data Model for our database, open a command window and type in the following:

```
edmgen /mode:fullgeneration /c:"Data Source=.;Initial
Catalog=Payroll;User ID=sa;Password=joydip1@3;" /p:Payroll
```

This will create a full ADO.NET Entity Data Model for our database. The output is shown in the following figure:

```
C:\test>edmgen /mode:fullgeneration /c:"Data Source=.;Initial Catalog=Payroll;Us
er ID=sa;Password=joydip1@3;" /p:Payroll
Microsoft (R) EdmGen version 3.5.0.0
Copyright (C) Microsoft Corporation 2007. All rights reserved.

Loading database information...
Writing ssdl file...
Creating conceptual layer from storage layer...
Writing msl file...
Writing csdl file...
Writing object layer file...
Writing views file...

Generation Complete -- 0 errors, 0 warnings

C:\test>
```

Getting Started

You can now see the list of the files that have been generated:

```
C:\test>edmgen /mode:fullgeneration /c:"Data Source=.;Initial Catalog=Payroll;User ID=sa;Password=joydip1@3;" /p:Payroll
Microsoft (R) EdmGen version 3.5.0.0
Copyright (C) Microsoft Corporation 2007. All rights reserved.

Loading database information...
Writing ssdl file...
Creating conceptual layer from storage layer...
Writing msl file...
Writing csdl file...
Writing object layer file...
Writing views file...

Generation Complete -- 0 errors, 0 warnings

C:\test>dir
 Volume in drive C has no label.
 Volume Serial Number is C8F9-748A

 Directory of C:\test

07/07/2008  11:14 AM    <DIR>          .
07/07/2008  11:14 AM    <DIR>          ..
07/07/2008  11:14 AM             7,177 Payroll.csdl
07/07/2008  11:14 AM             5,165 Payroll.msl
07/07/2008  11:14 AM            58,815 Payroll.ObjectLayer.cs
07/07/2008  11:14 AM             9,937 Payroll.ssdl
07/07/2008  11:14 AM            22,331 Payroll.Views.cs
               5 File(s)        103,425 bytes
               2 Dir(s)  57,760,059,392 bytes free

C:\test>
```

You can validate the Payroll Entity Data Model that was just created, using the `ValidateArtifacts` option of the EdmGen command line tool as shown below:

EdmGen /mode:ValidateArtifacts /inssdl:Payroll.ssdl /inmsl:Payroll.msl / incsdl:Payroll.csdl

When you execute the above command, the output will be similar to what is shown in the following figure:

```
C:\test>EdmGen /mode:ValidateArtifacts /inssdl:Payroll.ssdl /inmsl:Payroll.msl /incsdl:Payroll.csdl
Microsoft (R) EdmGen version 3.5.0.0
Copyright (C) Microsoft Corporation 2007. All rights reserved.

Validation Complete -- 0 errors, 0 warnings

C:\test>
```

As you can see in the previous figure, there are no warnings or errors displayed. So, our Entity Data Model is perfect.

The section that follows discusses the new Entity Data Source control which was introduced as part of the Visual Studio.NET 2008 SP1 release.

The ADO.NET Entity Data Source Control

Data controls are those that can be bound to data from external data sources. These data sources may include databases, XML files, or even flat files. ASP.NET 2.0 introduced some data source controls with a powerful data binding technique so the need for writing lengthy code for binding data to data controls has been eliminated.

> In ASP.NET, the term Data Binding implies binding the controls to data retrieved from a data source and providing a read or write connectivity between these controls and the data that they are bound to.

The Entity Data Source control is an example of a data control that is included as part of the Visual Studio 2008 SP1 release and can be used to bind data retrieved from an Entity Data Model to the data bound controls of ASP.NET. If you have installed Visual Studio 2008 SP1, you can see the EntityDataSource control listed in the Data section of your toolbox.

If you cannot locate the EntityDataSource control in the toolbox, follow these steps:

1. Right-click on the **Toolbox** and select the **Choose Items** option as shown in the following figure:

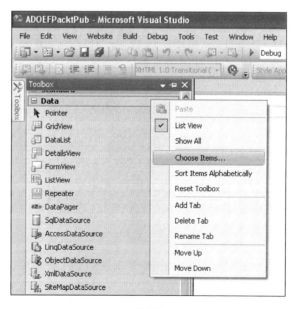

Getting Started

2. From the list of the components displayed, scroll down to locate the EntityDataSource in the .NET Framework Components tab. Refer to the following figure:

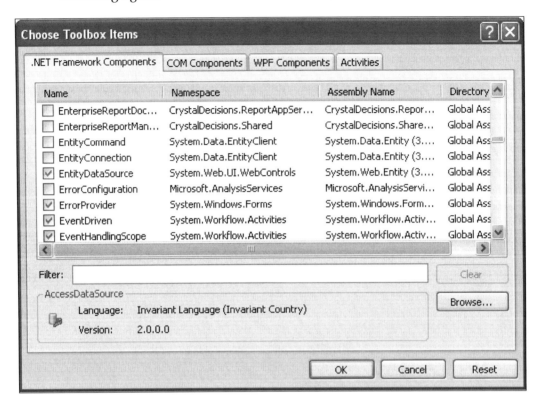

3. Now, check the checkbox next to the EntityDataSource component and click on **OK**.

Chapter 2

The ADO.NET Entity Data Source control is now added to your toolbox as shown in the following figure:

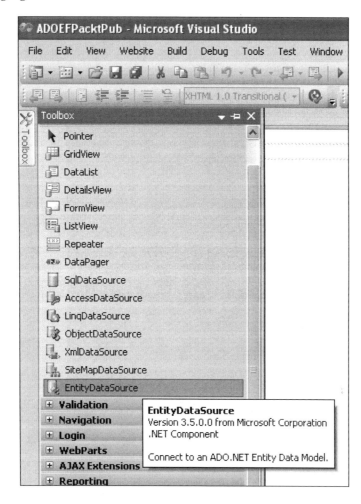

If the EntityDataSource component is not listed in the list of the components displayed in the Choose Toolbox Items window, you will have to add it manually. To do this, click on the **Browse** button in the Choose Toolbox Items window, locate the `System.Web.Entity.dll` in the folder in your system where Microsoft .NET Framework 3.5 has been installed and click on **OK**.

Getting Started

Implementing Our First Application Using the Entity Framework

In this section, we will learn how to use the Entity Data Model and the Entity Data Source Control to implement our first program using the Entity Framework. We will use a GridView control to display bound data.

Refer to the solution we created earlier using the Entity Data Model Designer. Now, follow these steps:

1. Drag and drop an Entity Data Source control from the toolbox onto your Default.aspx web form.

2. Now, click on the **Configure Data Source** option to specify the data source. Refer to the following figure:

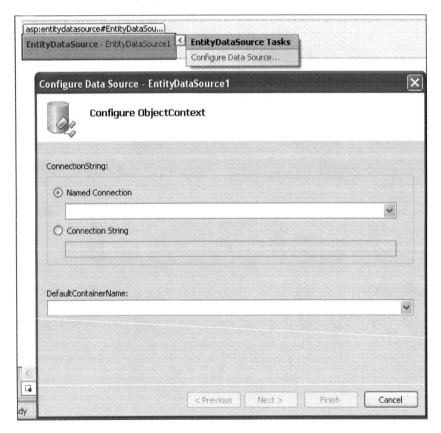

3. Specify the Connection String and DefaultContainerName and then click on **Next**.

Chapter 2

4. Specify the fields you would want to retrieve from the database table and click on **Finish** when done.
5. Now, drag and drop a **GridView** control from the toolbox onto the `Default.aspx` web form as seen in the following figure:

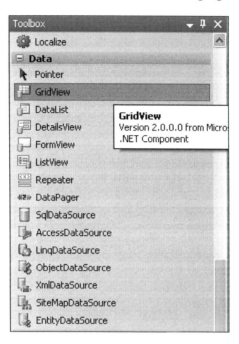

6. Next, use the **Choose Data Source** option of the GridView control to associate its data source with the Entity Data Source control we created earlier. Refer to the following figure:

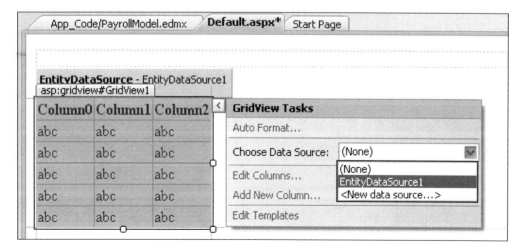

[55]

Here is how the markup code of the GridView control looks with its templates defined. Note how the DataSourceID of the GridView control has been associated with the Entity Data Source control we created earlier.

```
<asp:GridView ID="GridView1" runat="server" AutoGenerateColumns=
"False" DataKeyNames="EmployeeID"
    DataSourceID="SqlDataSource1" BorderColor="Black"
BorderStyle="Solid" Width="400px">
        <Columns>
            <asp:BoundField DataField="EmployeeID"
HeaderText="Employee ID" ReadOnly="True" SortExpression="EmployeeID"
/>
            <asp:BoundField DataField="FirstName" HeaderText=
"First Name" SortExpression="FirstName" />
            <asp:BoundField DataField="LastName" HeaderText=
"Last Name" SortExpression="LastName" />
            <asp:BoundField DataField="Address" HeaderText="Address"
SortExpression="Address" />
        </Columns>
</asp:GridView>
```

We are done! When you execute the application, your output should be similar to what is shown in the following figure:

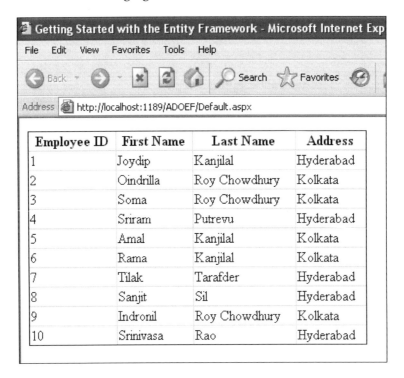

Summary

In this chapter, we have discussed how we can get started with the ADO.NET Entity Framework. We have learned how to create an Entity Data Model and use it along with the Entity Data Source control to bind data to a GridView data control. In the next chapter, we will continue to explore the Entity Data Model including each of its sections, and how they are related to each other.

3
Entities, Relationships, and the Entity Data Model

In the last chapter, we learned how we can get started using the ADO.NET Entity Framework. In this chapter, we will learn about the **ADO.NET Entity Data Model** and its components. The ADO.NET Entity Data Model is a conceptual model that can be used to design the data access layer of your application. We will revisit our Payroll Entity Data Model we created in the previous chapter and discuss each of the sections. Specifically, we will discuss the following points:

- An understanding of the entities, entity types, and relationships in the ADO.NET Entity Data Model
- An understanding of the Payroll Entity Data Model

We designed an EDM from our Payroll database in the previous chapter. In this chapter, we will discuss each of the sections of the EDM in detail. We will start our discussion with an understanding of entities and their relationships. We will then move ahead and discuss how they are mapped in the Entity Data Model using XML.

Entities, Entity Types, and Relationships in the ADO.NET Entity Data Model (EDM)

The Entity Data Model (EDM) is an implementation for the Entity-Relationship model (commonly called the E-R model). It depicts entities and their relationships. The **EDM** is a view of the data store that your application will use.

Before we delve deep into our Payroll EDM, let's have a discussion of entities, entity types, relationships, and how these are all represented.

What is an Entity?

An **Entity** essentially models individual, real-world objects like employees and customers. Such objects contain information pertaining to the entity. An entity is something that is uniquely definable, distinctly identifiable, and can have one or more of the following properties:

1. It should be easily identifiable through the data that it holds.
2. It should have properties that can hold scalar values that represent the entity's data.
3. It should only contain data, not methods or operations on the data.
4. It can have entity relationship information such as how one entity is related to another.

An entity refers to an instance of an **EntityType**, such as an Employee, a Customer, or a Product. The identity of an entity is defined using an EntityType. As an example, an Employee belongs to a particular Department; a Product belongs to a particular Group, a Customer buys a particular Product, etc. Each and every EntityType is uniquely identified by a unique key also called the **EntityKey**.

> The names of the nodes in the EDM, such as EntityKey and EntityType should not have any space in the middle. This is the convention for the XML syntax used in EDM.

Any two entities can be related to each other using relationships. These relationships are actually instances of **Relationship Types**. Such relationships can either be an **Association** or **Containment**.

Defining Entity Sets in the Entity Data Model

An **EntitySet** may be defined as a logical grouping of similar entities. In other words, all the entities contained within an EntitySet are of the same, or derived from the same, EntityType. Here is how an EntitySet is defined in the Entity Data Model:

```
<EntitySet Name="Employee" EntityType="PayrollModel.Employee" />
<EntitySet Name="Department" EntityType="PayrollModel.Department" />
<EntitySet Name="Salary" EntityType="PayrollModel.Salary" />
```

Note that the `EntityType` for the `EntitySets` are defined using the `EntityType` attribute. Fine, but what does an EntityType contain? An `EntityType` consists of one or more properties and a key. These properties can be non-nullable which implies that they are mandatory fields in the database.

Here is how an `EntityType` is defined in the Entity Data Model:

```xml
<EntityType Name="Salary">
  <Key>
    <PropertyRef Name="SalaryID" />
  </Key>
  <Property Name="SalaryID" Type="Int32" Nullable="false" />
  <Property Name="Basic" Type="Decimal" Nullable="false" Precision="19" Scale="4" />
  <Property Name="Allowance" Type="Decimal" Nullable="false" Precision="19" Scale="4" />
  <Property Name="Tax" Type="Decimal" Nullable="false" Precision="19" Scale="4" />
  <Property Name="GrossSalary" Type="Decimal" Nullable="false" Precision="19" Scale="4" />
  <Property Name="NetSalary" Type="Decimal" Nullable="false" Precision="19" Scale="4" />
  <NavigationProperty Name="Employee" Relationship="PayrollModel.FK_Salary_Employee" FromRole="Salary" ToRole="Employee" />
  <NavigationProperty Name="ProvidentFund" Relationship="PayrollModel.FK_Salary_ProvidentFund" FromRole="Salary" ToRole="ProvidentFund" />
</EntityType>
```

Note how the `Name` attribute and the `Key` element of the `EntityType` are defined. The property names of the Entity are defined using the `Property` elements. Each of these properties has specified types such as integers or strings. The `Nullable` attribute is used to denote whether or not the property can accept null values. It is a boolean attribute and accepts either a true or false value. A `NavigationProperty` is one that defines the end points of a relationship. If you look at the above code snippet that illustrates the `Salary EntityType`, you will find two navigation properties, namely, `Employee` and `ProvidentFund`. While the former is used to represent the association between the `Salary` and `Employee` entities, the latter is used to represent the association between the `Salary` and `ProvidentFund` entities in the EDM.

Extending the Existing Entity Types to Create Derived Entity Types

The EDM allows you to derive a type from a base type. The derived type extends an existing entity type to add additional information specific to the type. The EDM also allows you to specify multiple derived types, also called sub types, from a common base type. As an example, both `Employee` and `Customer` can derive from the base type called `Person`. These sub types then in turn be the base types for other entities. So, the `Employee` type can in turn be the base type for `Manager`, and so on.

Here is how you can extend an existing EntityType to specify your own derived Entitytype:

```
<EntityType Name="Manager" BaseType="Employee">
        <Property Name="Role" Type="System.String" Size="max" />
</EntityType>
```

 You cannot implement methods in the EDM, hence, method inheritance is not supported.

In the EDM, you can specify inheritance in two ways:

- Table-per-Hierarchy Model
- Table-per-Type Model

In the Table-per-Hierarchy Model, the base types and the derived types are all specified using the same database table. In the Table-per-Type Model, the base type is in one table while the derived types are spread across other tables.

Association Sets, Associations, Containment, and Multiplicity

A relationship represents the logical connection between two or more entities. The EDM supports both unary and binary relationships. The **Association** type of relationship models the peer to peer connection between entities. In other words, it links two or more entities. It has a name and some elements that define the endpoints of the association.

Let us consider the EmployeeSalary entity. An Employee may belong to a specific Department, where Department is another entity. To relate, we will require a key such as DepartmentID. We can then use this key to relate the Employee and Department entities.

An **AssociationSet** is a set of associations. While an Association and an Entity represent the types, an AssociationSet and an EntitySet represent the storage location of those types. Association and AssociationSet information provides information to the EntityFramework on how to construct collections of instances at runtime.

Here is how an **AssociationSet** is defined in the Entity Data Model:

```
<Association Name="FK_Employee_Department">
        <End Role="Department" Type="PayrollModel.Department" Multiplicity="1" />
        <End Role="Employee" Type="PayrollModel.Employee" Multiplicity="*" />
</Association>
<Association Name="FK_Salary_Employee">
        <End Role="Employee" Type="PayrollModel.Employee" Multiplicity="1" />
        <End Role="Salary" Type="PayrollModel.Salary" Multiplicity="*" />
</Association>
```

Containment is a type of bidirectional relationship with the multiplicity as 1 to 0..N. Here is an example of how a Containment relationship is defined in the Entity Data Model:

```
<Containment Name="Parent_Child">
   <End Type="Parent" role="Parent" />
   <End Type="Child" Multiplicity="*" role="Children" />
</Containment>
```

Multiplicity is used to define the number of entity instances that are related to the other. Based on multiplicity, relationships between entities can be one of the following:

- One-to-one
- One-to-many
- Many-to-many

The **Multiplicity** attribute as shown in the above code snippet, is used to define one to one, one to many or many to many relations amongst the entities.

What are Entity Containers?

All EntitySets and AssociationSets are defined within the context of the **Entity Container** which is a logical grouping of EntitySets and RelationshipSets. Here is an example of how an **EntityContainer** is defined in EDM:

```
<EntityContainer Name="PayrollEntities">
        <EntitySet Name="Employee" EntityType="PayrollModel.Employee" />
        <EntitySet Name="Department" EntityType="PayrollModel.Department" />
```

Entities, Relationships, and the Entity Data Model

```
            <EntitySet Name="Salary" EntityType="PayrollModel.Salary" />
            <AssociationSet Name="FK_Employee_Department" Association="P
ayrollModel.FK_Employee_Department">
                <End Role="Department" EntitySet="Department" />
                <End Role="Employee" EntitySet="Employee" />
            </AssociationSet>
            <AssociationSet Name="FK_Salary_Employee" Association="Payro
llModel.FK_Salary_Employee">
                <End Role="Employee" EntitySet="Employee" />
                <End Role="Salary" EntitySet="Salary" />
            </AssociationSet>
        </EntityContainer>
```

In the next section, we will revisit the Payroll Entity Data Model created in the previous chapter and take a look at its components (CSDL, MSL, and SSDL sections).

Exploring the Payroll Entity Data Model

The ADO.NET Entity Data Model allows the application to have its own view of the application's data.

Here again is the design view of the Payroll EDM we created in Chapter 2:

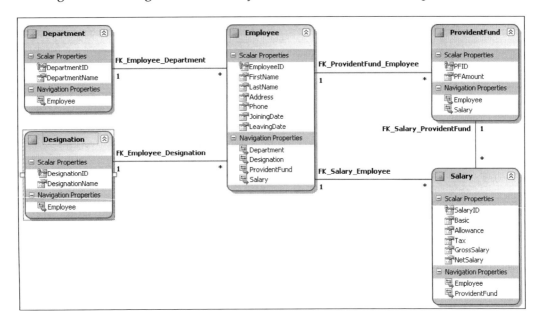

Note that the relationships and the respective fields are displayed along with their multiplicity. You can also see the Scalar and NavigationProperties. While the Scalar Properties section lists the attributes or the fields of the Entity, the NavigationProperties are those that denote the associations of a particular Entity with other entities. As an example, the Employee entity uses the Department and the Salary entities to relate its foreign keys DepartmentID and SalaryID respectively. Therefore, you can see that the Department and Salary entities are listed in the NavigationProperties section of the Employee entity.

The Mapping Details Window

Now we will take a look at the mappings details. That is, how the properties of the entities are mapped to the underlying database.

To do this, select any entity in the Entity Data Model in the design view, right-click on it, and then click on the **Show in Mapping Details** option as shown in the following figure:

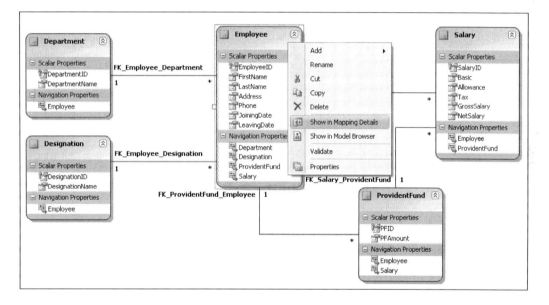

Here is how the Mapping Details of the Employee entity looks:

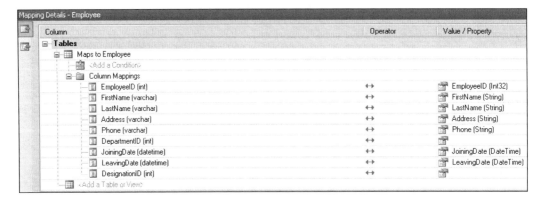

Here is how the Mapping Details for the Department entity looks:

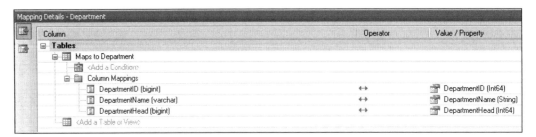

Here is how the Mapping Details for the Designation entity looks:

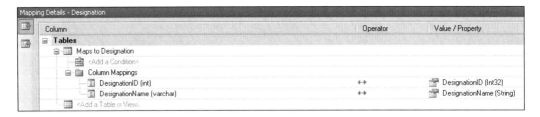

Here is how the Mapping Details for the Provident Fund entity looks:

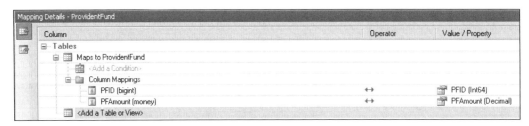

Here is how the Mapping Details for the Salary entity looks:

The Entity Model Browser

The **Entity Model Browser** shows the conceptual and storage models of your Entity Data Model in a diagram view. When you open an Entity Data Model in the Model Browser, you can see the following:

- The Conceptual Model
    - Entity Types
    - Associations
    - Entity Container
    - Entity Sets
    - Association Sets
    - Function Imports

- The Storage Model
    - Tables
    - Views
    - Stored Procedures
    - Constraints

Here is how the Payroll EDM looks when opened in the **Model Browser**:

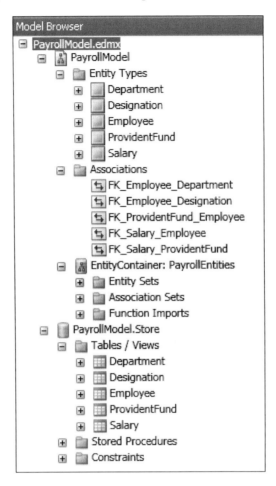

As you can see from the above figure, we have the **EDM** and its entity types, the Associations, and also the Store where we have our database tables, views, stored procedures, and constraints.

The Entity Data Model Layers

Now, when you open our Payroll **EDM** file in its XML view, you can see three major sections including

- The Conceptual Model (CSDL)
- The Storage Model (SSDL)
- The Mapping Layer (MSL)

In the sections that follow, we will take a look at each of these sections of our Payroll Data Model.

The CSDL Schema

The Entity Data Model uses the **Conceptual Schema Definition Language** to define Entities and their relationships. The CSDL Schema defines a namespace and an alias that can be used for referencing. The **CSDL** content comprises mainly of:

- An Entity Container
- A collection of EntityTypes
- A collection of Associations

The CSDL schema is organized as a collection of EntitySets, AssociationSets, EntityTypes, and AssociationTypes as shown below:

```
<EntityContainer>
    <EntitySet>
    <EntitySet/>

    <EntitySet>
    <EntitySet/>

    <AssociationSet>
    </AssociationSet>

    <AssociationSet>
    </AssociationSet>
</EntityContainer>
<EntityType>
</EntityType>
<EntityType>
</EntityType>
<Association>
</Association>
<Association>
</Association>
```

We have an `EntityContainer` called `PayrollEntities`, a collection of `EntitySets` including `Employee`, `Department`, `Salary`, `Designation`, and `ProvidentFund`.

Here is how the `EntitySets` are organized:

```
<EntityContainer Name="PayrollEntities">
        <EntitySet Name="Employee" EntityType="PayrollModel.Employee" />
        <EntitySet Name="Department" EntityType="PayrollModel.Department" />
```

```xml
        <EntitySet Name="Designation" EntityType="PayrollModel.Designation" />
        <EntitySet Name="ProvidentFund" EntityType="PayrollModel.ProvidentFund" />
        <EntitySet Name="Salary" EntityType="PayrollModel.Salary" />
```

We also have a collection of EntityTypes with their properties and navigation properties defined. Here is an example:

```xml
        <EntityType Name="Employee">
          <Key>
            <PropertyRef Name="EmployeeID" />
          </Key>
          <Property Name="EmployeeID" Type="Int32" Nullable="false" />
          <Property Name="FirstName" Type="String" Nullable="false" MaxLength="50" Unicode="false" />
          <Property Name="LastName" Type="String" Nullable="false" MaxLength="50" Unicode="false" />
          <Property Name="Address" Type="String" Nullable="false" MaxLength="50" Unicode="false" />
          <Property Name="Phone" Type="String" Nullable="false" MaxLength="50" Unicode="false" />
          <Property Name="JoiningDate" Type="DateTime" Nullable="false" />
          <Property Name="LeavingDate" Type="DateTime" />
          <NavigationProperty Name="Department" Relationship="PayrollModel.FK_Employee_Department" FromRole="Employee" ToRole="Department" />
          <NavigationProperty Name="Designation" Relationship="PayrollModel.FK_Employee_Designation" FromRole="Employee" ToRole="Designation" />
          <NavigationProperty Name="ProvidentFund" Relationship="PayrollModel.FK_ProvidentFund_Employee" FromRole="Employee" ToRole="ProvidentFund" />
          <NavigationProperty Name="Salary" Relationship="PayrollModel.FK_Salary_Employee" FromRole="Employee" ToRole="Salary" />
        </EntityType>
```

Next we have several associations as shown below:

```xml
    <Association Name="FK_Employee_Department">
          <End Role="Department" Type="PayrollModel.Department" Multiplicity="1" />
          <End Role="Employee" Type="PayrollModel.Employee" Multiplicity="*" />
    </Association>
```

```xml
<Association Name="FK_Employee_Designation">
        <End Role="Designation" Type="PayrollModel.Designation" Multiplicity="0..1" />
        <End Role="Employee" Type="PayrollModel.Employee" Multiplicity="*" />
</Association>
<Association Name="FK_Employee_ProvidentFund">
        <End Role="ProvidentFund" Type="PayrollModel.ProvidentFund" Multiplicity="0..1" />
        <End Role="Employee" Type="PayrollModel.Employee" Multiplicity="*" />
</Association>
<Association Name="FK_Employee_Salary">
        <End Role="Salary" Type="PayrollModel.Salary" Multiplicity="1" />
        <End Role="Employee" Type="PayrollModel.Employee" Multiplicity="*" />
</Association>
```

You also have `AssociationSets` that comprise of a set of Association definitions with each association depicting a foreign key relation. Note that the `EndRole` attribute of the `AssociationSet` defines the end point of the foreign key relation.

Here is the how the `AssociationSets` are defined in our Payroll EDM:

```xml
<AssociationSet Name="FK_Employee_Department" Association="PayrollModel.FK_Employee_Department">
        <End Role="Department" EntitySet="Department" />
        <End Role="Employee" EntitySet="Employee" />
</AssociationSet>
<AssociationSet Name="FK_Employee_Designation" Association="PayrollModel.FK_Employee_Designation">
        <End Role="Designation" EntitySet="Designation" />
        <End Role="Employee" EntitySet="Employee" />
</AssociationSet>
<AssociationSet Name="FK_Employee_ProvidentFund" Association="PayrollModel.FK_Employee_ProvidentFund">
        <End Role="ProvidentFund" EntitySet="ProvidentFund" />
        <End Role="Employee" EntitySet="Employee" />
</AssociationSet>
<AssociationSet Name="FK_Employee_Salary" Association="PayrollModel.FK_Employee_Salary">
        <End Role="Salary" EntitySet="Salary" />
        <End Role="Employee" EntitySet="Employee" />
</AssociationSet>
```

Entities, Relationships, and the Entity Data Model

As you can see from the above code snippet, the `AssociationSet` called `FK_Employee_Department` defines a foreign key relation between the `Employee` and `Department` entities:

Here is the complete CSDL Schema of the Payroll EDM for your reference:

```xml
<!-- CSDL content -->
    <edmx:ConceptualModels>
      <Schema Namespace="PayrollModel" Alias="Self" xmlns=
"http://schemas.microsoft.com/ado/2006/04/edm">
        <EntityContainer Name="PayrollEntities">
          <EntitySet Name="Department" EntityType="PayrollModel.
Department" />
          <EntitySet Name="Designation" EntityType="PayrollModel.
Designation" />
          <EntitySet Name="Employee" EntityType="PayrollModel.
Employee" />
          <EntitySet Name="ProvidentFund" EntityType="PayrollModel.
ProvidentFund" />
          <EntitySet Name="Salary" EntityType="PayrollModel.Salary" />
          <AssociationSet Name="FK_Employee_Department" Association=
"PayrollModel.FK_Employee_Department">
            <End Role="Department" EntitySet="Department" />
            <End Role="Employee" EntitySet="Employee" />
          </AssociationSet>
          <AssociationSet Name="FK_Employee_Designation" Association=
"PayrollModel.FK_Employee_Designation">
            <End Role="Designation" EntitySet="Designation" />
            <End Role="Employee" EntitySet="Employee" />
          </AssociationSet>
          <AssociationSet Name="FK_ProvidentFund_Employee" Association
="PayrollModel.FK_ProvidentFund_Employee">
            <End Role="Employee" EntitySet="Employee" />
            <End Role="ProvidentFund" EntitySet="ProvidentFund" />
          </AssociationSet>
          <AssociationSet Name="FK_Salary_Employee" Association=
"PayrollModel.FK_Salary_Employee">
            <End Role="Employee" EntitySet="Employee" />
            <End Role="Salary" EntitySet="Salary" />
          </AssociationSet>
          <AssociationSet Name="FK_Salary_ProvidentFund" Association=
"PayrollModel.FK_Salary_ProvidentFund">
            <End Role="ProvidentFund" EntitySet="ProvidentFund" />
            <End Role="Salary" EntitySet="Salary" />
          </AssociationSet>
        </EntityContainer>
```

```xml
<EntityType Name="Department">
  <Key>
    <PropertyRef Name="DepartmentID" />
  </Key>
  <Property Name="DepartmentID" Type="Int32" Nullable="false" />
  <Property Name="DepartmentName" Type="String" Nullable="false" MaxLength="50" Unicode="false" />
  <NavigationProperty Name="Employee" Relationship="PayrollModel.FK_Employee_Department" FromRole="Department" ToRole="Employee" />
</EntityType>
<EntityType Name="Designation">
  <Key>
    <PropertyRef Name="DesignationID" />
  </Key>
  <Property Name="DesignationID" Type="Int32" Nullable="false" />
  <Property Name="DesignationName" Type="String" Nullable="false" MaxLength="50" Unicode="false" />
  <NavigationProperty Name="Employee" Relationship="PayrollModel.FK_Employee_Designation" FromRole="Designation" ToRole="Employee" />
</EntityType>
<EntityType Name="Employee">
  <Key>
    <PropertyRef Name="EmployeeID" />
  </Key>
  <Property Name="EmployeeID" Type="Int32" Nullable="false" />
  <Property Name="FirstName" Type="String" Nullable="false" MaxLength="50" Unicode="false" />
  <Property Name="LastName" Type="String" Nullable="false" MaxLength="50" Unicode="false" />
  <Property Name="Address" Type="String" Nullable="false" MaxLength="50" Unicode="false" />
  <Property Name="Phone" Type="String" Nullable="false" MaxLength="50" Unicode="false" />
  <Property Name="JoiningDate" Type="DateTime" Nullable="false" />
  <Property Name="LeavingDate" Type="DateTime" />
  <NavigationProperty Name="Department" Relationship="PayrollModel.FK_Employee_Department" FromRole="Employee" ToRole="Department" />
  <NavigationProperty Name="Designation" Relationship="PayrollModel.FK_Employee_Designation" FromRole="Employee" ToRole="Designation" />
```

```xml
        <NavigationProperty Name="ProvidentFund" Relationship=
"PayrollModel.FK_ProvidentFund_Employee" FromRole="Employee"
ToRole="ProvidentFund" />
        <NavigationProperty Name="Salary" Relationship=
"PayrollModel.FK_Salary_Employee" FromRole="Employee" ToRole=
"Salary" />
      </EntityType>
      <EntityType Name="ProvidentFund">
        <Key>
          <PropertyRef Name="PFID" />
        </Key>
        <Property Name="PFID" Type="Int32" Nullable="false" />
        <Property Name="PFAmount" Type="Decimal" Nullable="false"
Precision="19" Scale="4" />
        <NavigationProperty Name="Employee" Relationship=
"PayrollModel.FK_ProvidentFund_Employee" FromRole="ProvidentFund"
ToRole="Employee" />
        <NavigationProperty Name="Salary" Relationship="PayrollModel
.FK_Salary_ProvidentFund" FromRole="ProvidentFund" ToRole="Salary" />
      </EntityType>
      <EntityType Name="Salary">
        <Key>
          <PropertyRef Name="SalaryID" />
        </Key>
        <Property Name="SalaryID" Type="Int32" Nullable="false" />
        <Property Name="Basic" Type="Decimal" Nullable="false"
Precision="19" Scale="4" />
        <Property Name="Allowance" Type="Decimal" Nullable="false"
Precision="19" Scale="4" />
        <Property Name="Tax" Type="Decimal" Nullable="false"
Precision="19" Scale="4" />
        <Property Name="GrossSalary" Type="Decimal" Nullable="false"
Precision="19" Scale="4" />
        <Property Name="NetSalary" Type="Decimal" Nullable="false"
Precision="19" Scale="4" />
        <NavigationProperty Name="Employee" Relationship=
"PayrollModel.FK_Salary_Employee" FromRole="Salary" ToRole=
"Employee" />
        <NavigationProperty Name="ProvidentFund" Relationship=
"PayrollModel.FK_Salary_ProvidentFund" FromRole="Salary"
ToRole="ProvidentFund" />
      </EntityType>
      <Association Name="FK_Employee_Department">
        <End Role="Department" Type="PayrollModel.Department"
Multiplicity="1" />
        <End Role="Employee" Type="PayrollModel.Employee"
Multiplicity="*" />
```

```xml
        </Association>
        <Association Name="FK_Employee_Designation">
          <End Role="Designation" Type="PayrollModel.Designation" Multiplicity="1" />
          <End Role="Employee" Type="PayrollModel.Employee" Multiplicity="*" />
        </Association>
        <Association Name="FK_ProvidentFund_Employee">
          <End Role="Employee" Type="PayrollModel.Employee" Multiplicity="1" />
          <End Role="ProvidentFund" Type="PayrollModel.ProvidentFund" Multiplicity="*" />
        </Association>
        <Association Name="FK_Salary_Employee">
          <End Role="Employee" Type="PayrollModel.Employee" Multiplicity="1" />
          <End Role="Salary" Type="PayrollModel.Salary" Multiplicity="*" />
        </Association>
        <Association Name="FK_Salary_ProvidentFund">
          <End Role="ProvidentFund" Type="PayrollModel.ProvidentFund" Multiplicity="1" />
          <End Role="Salary" Type="PayrollModel.Salary" Multiplicity="*" />
        </Association>
      </Schema>
    </edmx:ConceptualModels>
```

In the next section, we will take a look at the SSDL section in the Payroll EDM.

The SSDL Schema

The schema definition for the SSDL section is similar to its CSDL counterpart. In addition to what we have just seen in the CSDL schema, we have field types, field lengths, and Identity properties that specify whether a particular column in the database table is an identity column. We also have key columns and a collection of Functions that relate to the Stored Procedures that were defined earlier in our Payroll database.

Entities, Relationships, and the Entity Data Model

The SSDL schema is also organized much the same as CSDL with the relational schema information of the database in use. Here is how the Employee entity is represented in SSDL:

```xml
<EntityType Name="Employee">
  <Key>
    <PropertyRef Name="EmployeeID" />
  </Key>
  <Property Name="EmployeeID" Type="int" Nullable="false" StoreGeneratedPattern="Identity" />
  <Property Name="FirstName" Type="varchar" Nullable="false" MaxLength="50" />
  <Property Name="LastName" Type="varchar" Nullable="false" MaxLength="50" />
  <Property Name="Address" Type="varchar" Nullable="false" MaxLength="50" />
  <Property Name="Phone" Type="varchar" Nullable="false" MaxLength="50" />
  <Property Name="DepartmentID" Type="int" Nullable="false" />
  <Property Name="JoiningDate" Type="datetime" Nullable="false" />
  <Property Name="LeavingDate" Type="datetime" />
  <Property Name="DesignationID" Type="int" Nullable="false" />
</EntityType>
```

As you can see from the above code snippet, relational schema information of the Employee entity has been represented in XML.

And here is the complete **SSDL** section of our Payroll EDM:

```xml
<!-- SSDL content -->
<edmx:StorageModels>
  <Schema Namespace="PayrollModel.Store" Alias="Self" ProviderManifestToken="09.00.1399" xmlns="http://schemas.microsoft.com/ado/2006/04/edm/ssdl">
    <EntityContainer Name="dbo">
      <EntitySet Name="Department" EntityType="PayrollModel.Store.Department" />
      <EntitySet Name="Designation" EntityType="PayrollModel.Store.Designation" />
      <EntitySet Name="Employee" EntityType="PayrollModel.Store.Employee" />
      <EntitySet Name="ProvidentFund" EntityType="PayrollModel.Store.ProvidentFund" />
      <EntitySet Name="Salary" EntityType="PayrollModel.Store.Salary" />
```

```xml
        <AssociationSet Name="FK_Employee_Department" Association=
"PayrollModel.Store.FK_Employee_Department">
            <End Role="Department" EntitySet="Department" />
            <End Role="Employee" EntitySet="Employee" />
        </AssociationSet>
        <AssociationSet Name="FK_Employee_Designation" Association=
"PayrollModel.Store.FK_Employee_Designation">
            <End Role="Designation" EntitySet="Designation" />
            <End Role="Employee" EntitySet="Employee" />
        </AssociationSet>
        <AssociationSet Name="FK_ProvidentFund_Employee" Association
="PayrollModel.Store.FK_ProvidentFund_Employee">
            <End Role="Employee" EntitySet="Employee" />
            <End Role="ProvidentFund" EntitySet="ProvidentFund" />
        </AssociationSet>
        <AssociationSet Name="FK_Salary_Employee" Association=
"PayrollModel.Store.FK_Salary_Employee">
            <End Role="Employee" EntitySet="Employee" />
            <End Role="Salary" EntitySet="Salary" />
        </AssociationSet>
        <AssociationSet Name="FK_Salary_ProvidentFund" Association=
"PayrollModel.Store.FK_Salary_ProvidentFund">
            <End Role="ProvidentFund" EntitySet="ProvidentFund" />
            <End Role="Salary" EntitySet="Salary" />
        </AssociationSet>
      </EntityContainer>
      <EntityType Name="Department">
        <Key>
          <PropertyRef Name="DepartmentID" />
        </Key>
        <Property Name="DepartmentID" Type="int" Nullable="false"
StoreGeneratedPattern="Identity" />
        <Property Name="DepartmentName" Type="varchar"
Nullable="false" MaxLength="50" />
      </EntityType>
      <EntityType Name="Designation">
        <Key>
          <PropertyRef Name="DesignationID" />
        </Key>
        <Property Name="DesignationID" Type="int" Nullable="false"
StoreGeneratedPattern="Identity" />
        <Property Name="DesignationName" Type="varchar"
Nullable="false" MaxLength="50" />
      </EntityType>
      <EntityType Name="Employee">
```

```xml
      <Key>
        <PropertyRef Name="EmployeeID" />
      </Key>
      <Property Name="EmployeeID" Type="int" Nullable="false" StoreGeneratedPattern="Identity" />
      <Property Name="FirstName" Type="varchar" Nullable="false" MaxLength="50" />
      <Property Name="LastName" Type="varchar" Nullable="false" MaxLength="50" />
      <Property Name="Address" Type="varchar" Nullable="false" MaxLength="50" />
      <Property Name="Phone" Type="varchar" Nullable="false" MaxLength="50" />
      <Property Name="DepartmentID" Type="int" Nullable="false" />
      <Property Name="JoiningDate" Type="datetime" Nullable="false" />
      <Property Name="LeavingDate" Type="datetime" />
      <Property Name="DesignationID" Type="int" Nullable="false" />
    </EntityType>
    <EntityType Name="ProvidentFund">
      <Key>
        <PropertyRef Name="PFID" />
      </Key>
      <Property Name="PFID" Type="int" Nullable="false" StoreGeneratedPattern="Identity" />
      <Property Name="EmployeeID" Type="int" Nullable="false" />
      <Property Name="PFAmount" Type="money" Nullable="false" />
    </EntityType>
    <EntityType Name="Salary">
      <Key>
        <PropertyRef Name="SalaryID" />
      </Key>
      <Property Name="SalaryID" Type="int" Nullable="false" StoreGeneratedPattern="Identity" />
      <Property Name="EmployeeID" Type="int" Nullable="false" />
      <Property Name="PFID" Type="int" Nullable="false" />
      <Property Name="Basic" Type="money" Nullable="false" />
      <Property Name="Allowance" Type="money" Nullable="false" />
      <Property Name="Tax" Type="money" Nullable="false" />
      <Property Name="GrossSalary" Type="money" Nullable="false" />
      <Property Name="NetSalary" Type="money" Nullable="false" />
    </EntityType>
    <Association Name="FK_Employee_Department">
```

```xml
        <End Role="Department" Type="PayrollModel.Store.Department" Multiplicity="1" />
        <End Role="Employee" Type="PayrollModel.Store.Employee" Multiplicity="*" />
        <ReferentialConstraint>
          <Principal Role="Department">
            <PropertyRef Name="DepartmentID" />
          </Principal>
          <Dependent Role="Employee">
            <PropertyRef Name="DepartmentID" />
          </Dependent>
        </ReferentialConstraint>
      </Association>
      <Association Name="FK_Employee_Designation">
        <End Role="Designation" Type="PayrollModel.Store.Designation" Multiplicity="1" />
        <End Role="Employee" Type="PayrollModel.Store.Employee" Multiplicity="*" />
        <ReferentialConstraint>
          <Principal Role="Designation">
            <PropertyRef Name="DesignationID" />
          </Principal>
          <Dependent Role="Employee">
            <PropertyRef Name="DesignationID" />
          </Dependent>
        </ReferentialConstraint>
      </Association>
      <Association Name="FK_ProvidentFund_Employee">
        <End Role="Employee" Type="PayrollModel.Store.Employee" Multiplicity="1" />
        <End Role="ProvidentFund" Type="PayrollModel.Store.ProvidentFund" Multiplicity="*" />
        <ReferentialConstraint>
          <Principal Role="Employee">
            <PropertyRef Name="EmployeeID" />
          </Principal>
          <Dependent Role="ProvidentFund">
            <PropertyRef Name="EmployeeID" />
          </Dependent>
        </ReferentialConstraint>
      </Association>
      <Association Name="FK_Salary_Employee">
        <End Role="Employee" Type="PayrollModel.Store.Employee" Multiplicity="1" />
```

Entities, Relationships, and the Entity Data Model

```xml
            <End Role="Salary" Type="PayrollModel.Store.Salary"
Multiplicity="*" />
          <ReferentialConstraint>
            <Principal Role="Employee">
              <PropertyRef Name="EmployeeID" />
            </Principal>
            <Dependent Role="Salary">
              <PropertyRef Name="EmployeeID" />
            </Dependent>
          </ReferentialConstraint>
        </Association>
        <Association Name="FK_Salary_ProvidentFund">
          <End Role="ProvidentFund" Type="PayrollModel.Store.ProvidentFund" Multiplicity="1" />
          <End Role="Salary" Type="PayrollModel.Store.Salary"
Multiplicity="*" />
          <ReferentialConstraint>
            <Principal Role="ProvidentFund">
              <PropertyRef Name="PFID" />
            </Principal>
            <Dependent Role="Salary">
              <PropertyRef Name="PFID" />
            </Dependent>
          </ReferentialConstraint>
        </Association>
      </Schema>
    </edmx:StorageModels>
```

The MSL Schema

We will now take a look at the **MSL** schema that defines the C-S mapping which maps the conceptual model to the relational store. Here is the **MSL** schema for our Payroll **EDM**:

```xml
    <!-- C-S mapping content -->
    <edmx:Mappings>
        <Mapping Space="C-S" xmlns="urn:schemas-microsoft-com:windows:
storage:mapping:CS">
          <EntityContainerMapping StorageEntityContainer="dbo" CdmEntity
Container="PayrollEntities">
            <EntitySetMapping Name="Department">
              <EntityTypeMapping TypeName="IsTypeOf(PayrollModel.
Department)">
                <MappingFragment StoreEntitySet="Department">
```

```xml
                <ScalarProperty Name="DepartmentID" ColumnName=
"DepartmentID" />
                <ScalarProperty Name="DepartmentName" ColumnName=
"DepartmentName" />
              </MappingFragment>
            </EntityTypeMapping>
          </EntitySetMapping>
          <EntitySetMapping Name="Designation">
            <EntityTypeMapping TypeName="IsTypeOf(PayrollModel.
Designation)">
              <MappingFragment StoreEntitySet="Designation">
                <ScalarProperty Name="DesignationID" ColumnName=
"DesignationID" />
                <ScalarProperty Name="DesignationName" ColumnName=
"DesignationName" />
              </MappingFragment>
            </EntityTypeMapping>
          </EntitySetMapping>
          <EntitySetMapping Name="Employee">
            <EntityTypeMapping TypeName="IsTypeOf(PayrollModel.
Employee)">
              <MappingFragment StoreEntitySet="Employee">
                <ScalarProperty Name="EmployeeID"
ColumnName="EmployeeID" />
                <ScalarProperty Name="FirstName"
ColumnName="FirstName" />
                <ScalarProperty Name="LastName" ColumnName=
"LastName" />
                <ScalarProperty Name="Address" ColumnName="Address" />
                <ScalarProperty Name="Phone" ColumnName="Phone" />
                <ScalarProperty Name="JoiningDate"
ColumnName="JoiningDate" />
                <ScalarProperty Name="LeavingDate"
ColumnName="LeavingDate" />
              </MappingFragment>
            </EntityTypeMapping>
          </EntitySetMapping>
          <EntitySetMapping Name="ProvidentFund">
            <EntityTypeMapping TypeName="IsTypeOf(PayrollModel.
ProvidentFund)">
              <MappingFragment StoreEntitySet="ProvidentFund">
                <ScalarProperty Name="PFID" ColumnName="PFID" />
                <ScalarProperty Name="PFAmount" ColumnName=
"PFAmount" />
              </MappingFragment>
            </EntityTypeMapping>
```

```xml
        </EntitySetMapping>
        <EntitySetMapping Name="Salary">
          <EntityTypeMapping TypeName="IsTypeOf(PayrollModel.Salary)">
            <MappingFragment StoreEntitySet="Salary">
              <ScalarProperty Name="SalaryID" ColumnName="SalaryID" />
              <ScalarProperty Name="Basic" ColumnName="Basic" />
              <ScalarProperty Name="Allowance" ColumnName="Allowance" />
              <ScalarProperty Name="Tax" ColumnName="Tax" />
              <ScalarProperty Name="GrossSalary" ColumnName="GrossSalary" />
              <ScalarProperty Name="NetSalary" ColumnName="NetSalary" />
            </MappingFragment>
          </EntityTypeMapping>
        </EntitySetMapping>
        <AssociationSetMapping Name="FK_Employee_Department" TypeName="PayrollModel.FK_Employee_Department" StoreEntitySet="Employee">
          <EndProperty Name="Department">
            <ScalarProperty Name="DepartmentID" ColumnName="DepartmentID" />
          </EndProperty>
          <EndProperty Name="Employee">
            <ScalarProperty Name="EmployeeID" ColumnName="EmployeeID" />
          </EndProperty>
        </AssociationSetMapping>
        <AssociationSetMapping Name="FK_Employee_Designation" TypeName="PayrollModel.FK_Employee_Designation" StoreEntitySet="Employee">
          <EndProperty Name="Designation">
            <ScalarProperty Name="DesignationID" ColumnName="DesignationID" />
          </EndProperty>
          <EndProperty Name="Employee">
            <ScalarProperty Name="EmployeeID" ColumnName="EmployeeID" />
          </EndProperty>
        </AssociationSetMapping>
        <AssociationSetMapping Name="FK_ProvidentFund_Employee" TypeName="PayrollModel.FK_ProvidentFund_Employee" StoreEntitySet="ProvidentFund">
          <EndProperty Name="Employee">
```

```xml
                <ScalarProperty Name="EmployeeID" ColumnName="EmployeeID" />
              </EndProperty>
              <EndProperty Name="ProvidentFund">
                <ScalarProperty Name="PFID" ColumnName="PFID" />
              </EndProperty>
            </AssociationSetMapping>
            <AssociationSetMapping Name="FK_Salary_Employee" TypeName="PayrollModel.FK_Salary_Employee" StoreEntitySet="Salary">
              <EndProperty Name="Employee">
                <ScalarProperty Name="EmployeeID" ColumnName="EmployeeID" />
              </EndProperty>
              <EndProperty Name="Salary">
                <ScalarProperty Name="SalaryID" ColumnName="SalaryID" />
              </EndProperty>
            </AssociationSetMapping>
            <AssociationSetMapping Name="FK_Salary_ProvidentFund" TypeName="PayrollModel.FK_Salary_ProvidentFund" StoreEntitySet="Salary">
              <EndProperty Name="ProvidentFund">
                <ScalarProperty Name="PFID" ColumnName="PFID" />
              </EndProperty>
              <EndProperty Name="Salary">
                <ScalarProperty Name="SalaryID" ColumnName="SalaryID" />
              </EndProperty>
            </AssociationSetMapping>
          </EntityContainerMapping>
        </Mapping>
      </edmx:Mappings>
```

As you can see in the above MSL schema, the `EntityContainerMapping` attribute is used to indicate that the `StorageEntityContainer` is mapped to the conceptual model container called `PayrollEntities`.

But, how is this mapping achieved? It does this by mapping each **EntitySet** and **AssociationSet** to the corresponding elements in the data store. As an example, it uses the `StoreEntitySet` attribute to map a particular EntityType to the corresponding database table. There are also many `ScalarProperty` attributes that define how a particular property is mapped to its corresponding column name in the database table.

Entities, Relationships, and the Entity Data Model

Here is how the mapping information for the Employee entity is represented:

```
<EntitySetMapping Name="Employee">
  <EntityTypeMapping TypeName="IsTypeOf(PayrollModel.Employee)">
    <MappingFragment StoreEntitySet="Employee">
      <ScalarProperty Name="EmployeeID" ColumnName="EmployeeID" />
      <ScalarProperty Name="FirstName" ColumnName="FirstName" />
      <ScalarProperty Name="LastName" ColumnName="LastName" />
      <ScalarProperty Name="Address" ColumnName="Address" />
      <ScalarProperty Name="Phone" ColumnName="Phone" />
      <ScalarProperty Name="JoiningDate" ColumnName="JoiningDate" />
      <ScalarProperty Name="LeavingDate" ColumnName="LeavingDate" />
    </MappingFragment>
  </EntityTypeMapping>
```

The `EntityTypeMapping` attribute in the code snippet above is used to specify the type of the entity being represented. It is represented as Container.Entity where PayrollModel is the Container and Employee is the entity. The list of ScalarProperty attributes relates the properties of the Employee entity to the corresponding field names in the database table. In essence, the MSL schema maps the CSDL and SSDL sections of the EDM.

Summary

In this chapter, we have had a detailed look at the **EDM** and how each of its sections relate to each other. We discussed each of the sections of our Payroll EDM and how they are related. In the next chapter, we will discuss how we can use stored procedures with the EDM to perform CRUD operations.

4
Working with Stored Procedures in the Entity Data Model

In the previous chapter, we learned about the ADO.NET Entity Data Model (EDM), a conceptual model, that can be used to design the data access layer of your application. In this chapter, we will discuss how to map stored procedures in the EDM and use them in our applications. We will discuss the following points:

- Mapping Stored Procedures to Functions in the EDM
- Using Stored Procedures
- Mapping Stored Procedures that return Custom Entity Types

Mapping Stored Procedures to Functions in the EDM

Stored Procedures are represented as functions in the EDM. To use these functions, they should be mapped to a corresponding Insert, Update, or Delete operation on the entity. To do this, you need to first create a Function Import and then use the designer to create its mapping. In this section, we will learn how to create these Function Imports for our EDM.

Working with Stored Procedures in the Entity Data Model

To begin, let's refer to the Entity Data Model we created in chapter 2:

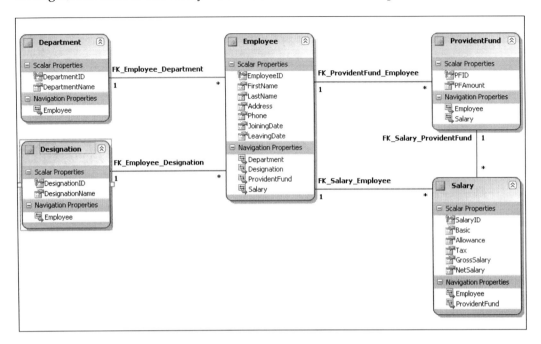

To create Function Imports, follow these steps:

1. Switch to the Model Browser of the Payroll Entity Data Model.
2. Expand the Entity Container and right click on **Function Imports** as shown in the following figure:

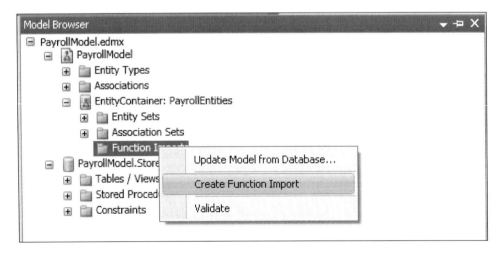

[86]

When you select **Create Function Import**, the New Function Import dialog appears and allows you to select the stored procedure you want from the list of available stored procedures. This is shown in the following figure:

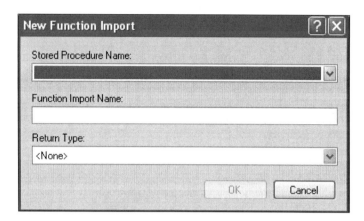

3. Now map the **Employee_Insert** stored procedure to a corresponding function import by selecting the Stored Procedure Name, the Function Import Name, and the Return Type. You can write the Function Import Name of your own choice.

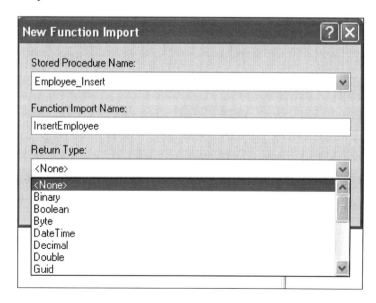

4. Repeat the above step to map the remaining procedures to their corresponding functions.

Working with Stored Procedures in the Entity Data Model

You can use the same procedure to map your select procedures. That is, procedures that return an entity or a collection of entities. The Return Type of such Function Imports should be the name of the entity in the EDM that it returns. As an example, here is how you can map the **GetAllEmployees** stored procedure using the New Function Import dialog window:

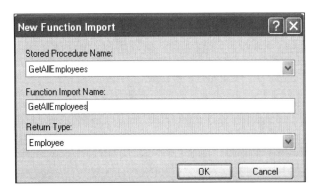

Once you are done mapping the procedures you need, you can see the complete list in the Model Browser:

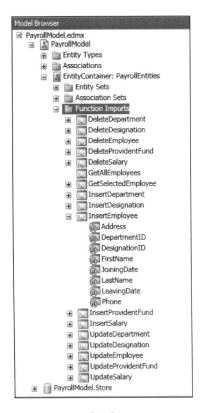

Chapter 4

Now that the Function Imports have been created, you need to map them to corresponding Insert, Update, and Delete operations on the entity using the designer.

Mapping Create, Update, and Delete Functions to Entities in the EDM

In this section, we will explore how to map the functions we just created to the corresponding entities of our EDM. Note that we need to map only the CUD functions. Refer to the Payroll EDM we created in Chapter 2.

Now, follow these steps:

1. Select the Employee entity, right-click on it and select **Show in Mapping Details** as shown in the following figure:

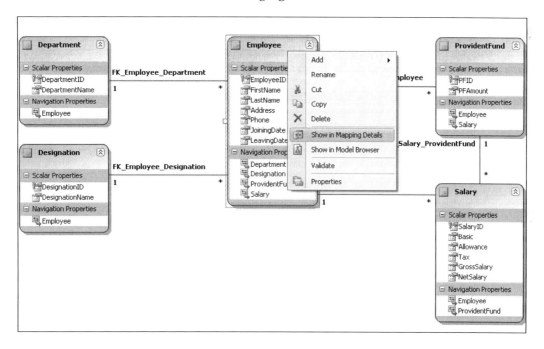

The Following screen will appear:

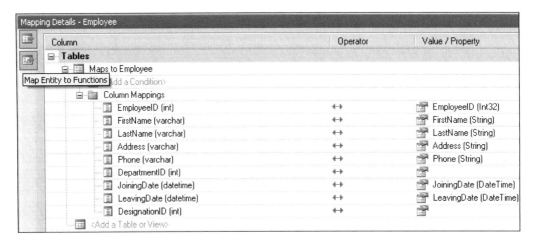

2. Click on **Map Entities to Functions** to map the CUD functions of the Employee entity as shown in the following figure:

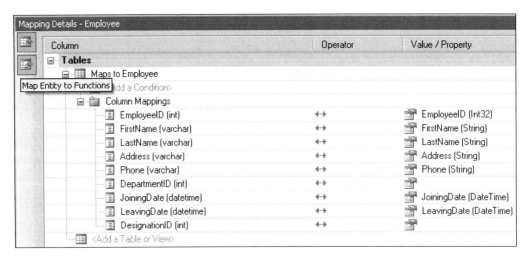

The following screen appears where you can specify the Insert, Update, and Delete functions for the Employee entity.

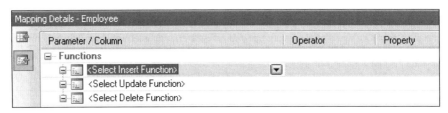

3. Click on the **Select Insert Function** drop down list to select the **Employee_Insert** function as the Insert function from the list of available functions for the Employee entity, as shown in the following figure:

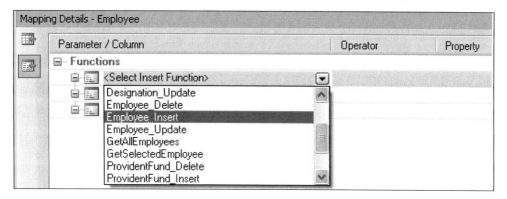

The Mapping Details window now displays the parameters and the corresponding properties to which they are bound as seen in the following figure:

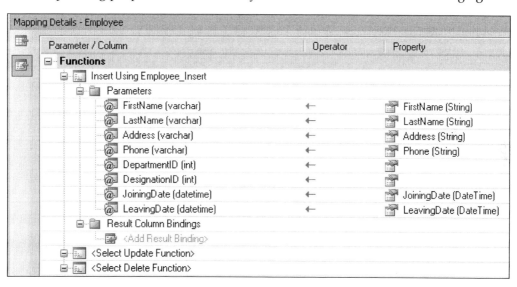

As you can see from the above figure, the field parameters and the field names of the Employee are mapped. You will need to manually map the **DepartmentID** and the **DesignationID** fields to the corresponding parameters as they are association mappings.

Working with Stored Procedures in the Entity Data Model

4. Now, click on the **DepartmentID** and **DesignationID** properties to map them to the corresponding parameters as shown below:

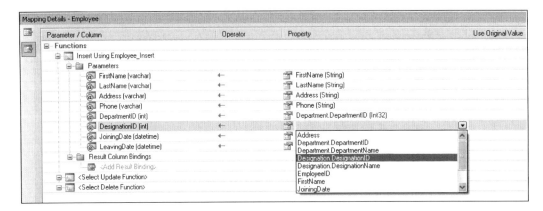

The Mapping Details window now reflects the mappings for the Insert function of the Employee entity:

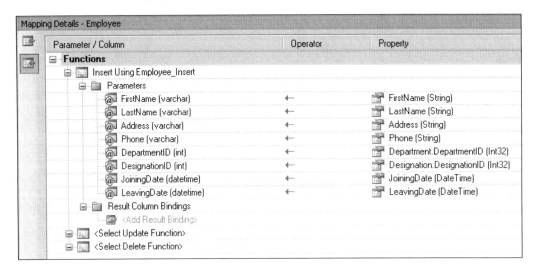

5. Repeat these steps to map the Update and Delete functions for the Employee entity.

If any of the entity sets or association sets in your data model uses function mappings, you will need to define function mappings for all related entity sets and association sets in the entity container which is a constraint indeed.

[92]

Mapping the Association Sets Consistently

Now that we have created the Function Imports and mapped them to the corresponding entities, let's compile the application once.

Oh no! When you compile the application, you will see a list of errors displayed:

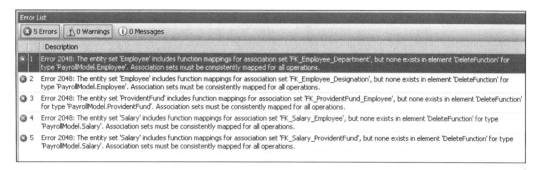

So, what went wrong? Are we missing something? Yes, the association sets in our EDM have not been mapped consistently.

There are certain rules that you should be aware of. If you are mapping stored procedures to entities in the EDM, with no associations or relationships, things are simple. You won't run into any problems. But, if your entities in the EDM have associations and relationships with other entities, you need to be careful.

When you are specifying an association in any one function mapping, you should do it for all other function mappings as well. So, a stored procedure that deletes an employee record should include a mapping specification for the Department entity as well.

So, what is the way out? Should we add an extra dummy parameter to our stored procedure that deletes an employee record? We can, but that's not a good choice. The other alternative is modifying the CSDL, SSDL, and MSL layers to add the extra parameter so the EDM is happy and no such errors are returned. Let's discuss how we can avoid such errors in the EDM.

Here is the list of the associations we have in our EDM:

```
<Association Name="FK_Employee_Department">
        <End Role="Department" Type="PayrollModel.Department" Multiplicity="1" />
        <End Role="Employee" Type="PayrollModel.Employee" Multiplicity="*" />
</Association>
<Association Name="FK_Employee_Designation">
```

Working with Stored Procedures in the Entity Data Model

```
            <End Role="Designation" Type="PayrollModel.Designation"
Multiplicity="1" />
            <End Role="Employee" Type="PayrollModel.Employee"
Multiplicity="*" />
</Association>
<Association Name="FK_ProvidentFund_Employee">
            <End Role="Employee" Type="PayrollModel.Employee"
Multiplicity="1" />
            <End Role="ProvidentFund" Type="PayrollModel.ProvidentFund"
Multiplicity="*" />
</Association>
<Association Name="FK_Salary_Employee">
            <End Role="Employee" Type="PayrollModel.Employee"
Multiplicity="1" />
            <End Role="Salary" Type="PayrollModel.Salary"
Multiplicity="*" />
</Association>
<Association Name="FK_Salary_ProvidentFund">
            <End Role="ProvidentFund" Type="PayrollModel.ProvidentFund"
Multiplicity="1" />
            <End Role="Salary" Type="PayrollModel.Salary"
Multiplicity="*" />
</Association>
```

You also have a list of Function Imports in the CSDL section. Let's take a look at the Function Imports for the Employee entity:

```
<FunctionImport Name="InsertEmployee">
<Parameter Name="FirstName" Mode="In" Type="String" />
<Parameter Name="LastName" Mode="In" Type="String" />
<Parameter Name="Address" Mode="In" Type="String" />
<Parameter Name="Phone" Mode="In" Type="String" />
<Parameter Name="DepartmentID" Mode="In" Type="Int32" />
<Parameter Name="DesignationID" Mode="In" Type="Int32" />
<Parameter Name="JoiningDate" Mode="In" Type="DateTime" />
<Parameter Name="LeavingDate" Mode="In" Type="DateTime" />
</FunctionImport>

<FunctionImport Name="UpdateEmployee"><Parameter Name="EmployeeID"
Mode="In" Type="Int32" />
<Parameter Name="FirstName" Mode="In" Type="String" />
<Parameter Name="LastName" Mode="In" Type="String" />
<Parameter Name="Address" Mode="In" Type="String" />
<Parameter Name="Phone" Mode="In" Type="String" />
<Parameter Name="DepartmentID" Mode="In" Type="Int32" />
<Parameter Name="DesignationID" Mode="In" Type="Int32" />
```

```
</FunctionImport>
<FunctionImport Name="DeleteEmployee">
<Parameter Name="EmployeeID" Mode="In" Type="Int32" />
</FunctionImport>
```

As you can see, the `DeleteEmployee FunctionImport` does not contain `DepartmentID` and `DesignationID` as parameters. Hence, you should specify `DepartmentID` and `DesignationID` as parameters to the `FunctionImport` called `DeleteEmployee` as shown below:

```
<FunctionImport Name="DeleteEmployee">
<Parameter Name="EmployeeID" Mode="In" Type="Int32" />
<Parameter Name="DepartmentID" Mode="In" Type="Int32" />
<Parameter Name="DesignationID" Mode="In" Type="Int32" />
</FunctionImport>
```

You should also add these parameters in the SSDL section.

```
<Function Name="Employee_Delete" Aggregate="false" BuiltIn="false"
NiladicFunction="false" IsComposable="false" ParameterTypeSemantics=
"AllowImplicitConversion" Schema="dbo">
<Parameter Name="EmployeeID" Type="int" Mode="In" />
<Parameter Name="DepartmentID" Type="int" Mode="In" />
<Parameter Name="DesignationID" Type="int" Mode="In" />
</Function>
```

In the C-S mapping section for the Employee entity, you can see the associations as shown below:

```
<ModificationFunctionMapping>
<InsertFunction FunctionName="PayrollModel.Store.Employee_Insert">
<ScalarProperty Name="LeavingDate" ParameterName="LeavingDate" />
<ScalarProperty Name="JoiningDate" ParameterName="JoiningDate" />
<ScalarProperty Name="Phone" ParameterName="Phone" />
<ScalarProperty Name="Address" ParameterName="Address" />
<ScalarProperty Name="LastName" ParameterName="LastName" />
<ScalarProperty Name="FirstName" ParameterName="FirstName" />
<AssociationEnd AssociationSet="FK_Employee_Department"
From="Employee" To="Department">
<ScalarProperty Name="DepartmentID" ParameterName="DepartmentID" />
</AssociationEnd>
<AssociationEnd AssociationSet="FK_Employee_Designation"
From="Employee" To="Designation">
<ScalarProperty Name="DesignationID" ParameterName="DesignationID" />
</AssociationEnd>
</InsertFunction>
```

Working with Stored Procedures in the Entity Data Model

```
<UpdateFunction FunctionName="PayrollModel.Store.Employee_Update">
<ScalarProperty Name="Phone" ParameterName="Phone" Version=
"Current" />
<ScalarProperty Name="Address" ParameterName="Address"
Version="Current" />
<ScalarProperty Name="LastName" ParameterName="LastName"
Version="Current" />
<ScalarProperty Name="FirstName" ParameterName="FirstName"
Version="Current" />
<ScalarProperty Name="EmployeeID" ParameterName="EmployeeID"
Version="Current" />
<AssociationEnd AssociationSet="FK_Employee_Department"
From="Employee" To="Department">
<ScalarProperty Name="DepartmentID" ParameterName="DepartmentID"
Version="Current" />
</AssociationEnd>
<AssociationEnd AssociationSet="FK_Employee_Designation"
From="Employee" To="Designation">
<ScalarProperty Name="DesignationID" ParameterName="DesignationID"
Version="Current" />
</AssociationEnd>
</UpdateFunction>
<DeleteFunction FunctionName="PayrollModel.Store.Employee_Delete">
<ScalarProperty Name="EmployeeID" ParameterName="EmployeeID" />
</DeleteFunction>
</ModificationFunctionMapping>
```

As you can see, the `DeleteFunction` called `Employee_Delete` doesn't contain the association mappings for `DepartmentID` and `DesignationID` properties. Let's add the associations for `FK_Employee_Department` and `FK_Employee_Designation` association sets in the `DeleteFunction` of the Employee entity now:

```
<DeleteFunction FunctionName="PayrollModel.Store.Employee_Delete">
<ScalarProperty Name="EmployeeID" ParameterName="EmployeeID" />
<AssociationEnd AssociationSet="FK_Employee_Department"
From="Employee" To="Department">
<ScalarProperty Name="DepartmentID" ParameterName="DepartmentID" />
</AssociationEnd>
<AssociationEnd AssociationSet="FK_Employee_Designation"
From="Employee" To="Designation">
<ScalarProperty Name="DesignationID" ParameterName="DesignationID" />
</AssociationEnd>
</DeleteFunction>
```

You need to do this for all the other associations as well. After you make the necessary changes, here is what the `FunctionImports` in the CSDL for `DeleteEmployee, DeleteDepartment, DeleteDesignation, DeleteProvidentFund`, and `DeleteSalary` look like:

```
<FunctionImport Name="DeleteEmployee">
        <Parameter Name="EmployeeID" Mode="In" Type="Int32" />
        <Parameter Name="DepartmentID" Mode="In" Type="Int32" />
        <Parameter Name="DesignationID" Mode="In" Type="Int32" />
</FunctionImport>

<FunctionImport Name="DeleteDepartment">
        <Parameter Name="DepartmentID" Mode="In" Type="Int32" />
</FunctionImport>

<FunctionImport Name="DeleteDesignation">
        <Parameter Name="DesignationID" Mode="In" Type="Int32" />
</FunctionImport>

<FunctionImport Name="DeleteProvidentFund">
        <Parameter Name="PFID" Mode="In" Type="Int32" />
        <Parameter Name="EmployeeID" Mode="In" Type="Int32" />
</FunctionImport>

<FunctionImport Name="DeleteSalary">
        <Parameter Name="SalaryID" Mode="In" Type="Int32" />
        <Parameter Name="EmployeeID" Mode="In" Type="Int32" />
        <Parameter Name="PFID" Mode="In" Type="Int32" />
</FunctionImport>
```

In the above code snippet, the required changes are in bolded text. Here is the list of their corresponding Functions in the SSDL:

```
<Function Name="Department_Delete" Aggregate="false" BuiltIn="false" NiladicFunction="false" IsComposable="false" ParameterTypeSemantics="AllowImplicitConversion" Schema="dbo">
        <Parameter Name="DepartmentID" Type="int" Mode="In" />
</Function>
<Function Name="Designation_Delete" Aggregate="false" BuiltIn="false" NiladicFunction="false" IsComposable="false" ParameterTypeSemantics="AllowImplicitConversion" Schema="dbo">
        <Parameter Name="DesignationID" Type="int" Mode="In" />
</Function>
<Function Name="Employee_Delete" Aggregate="false" BuiltIn="false" NiladicFunction="false" IsComposable="false" ParameterTypeSemantics="AllowImplicitConversion" Schema="dbo">
        <Parameter Name="EmployeeID" Type="int" Mode="In" />
        <Parameter Name="DepartmentID" Type="int" Mode="In" />
        <Parameter Name="DesignationID" Type="int" Mode="In" />
</Function>
```

Working with Stored Procedures in the Entity Data Model

```xml
<Function Name="ProvidentFund_Delete" Aggregate="false"
BuiltIn="false" NiladicFunction="false" IsComposable="false" Parameter
TypeSemantics="AllowImplicitConversion" Schema="dbo">
          <Parameter Name="PFID" Type="int" Mode="In" />
          <Parameter Name="EmployeeID" Type="int" Mode="In" />
</Function>
<Function Name="Salary_Delete" Aggregate="false" BuiltIn="false"
NiladicFunction="false" IsComposable="false" ParameterTypeSemantics="A
llowImplicitConversion" Schema="dbo">
          <Parameter Name="SalaryID" Type="int" Mode="In" />
          <Parameter Name="EmployeeID" Type="int" Mode="In" />
          <Parameter Name="PFID" Type="int" Mode="In" />
</Function>
```

And here is how the mapping information is specified in the MSL:

```xml
<DeleteFunction FunctionName="PayrollModel.Store.Employee_Delete">
          <ScalarProperty Name="EmployeeID" ParameterName=
"EmployeeID" />
          <AssociationEnd AssociationSet="FK_Employee_Department"
From="Employee" To="Department">
             <ScalarProperty Name="DepartmentID" ParameterName=
"DepartmentID" />
          </AssociationEnd>
          <AssociationEnd AssociationSet="FK_Employee_Designation"
From="Employee" To="Designation">
             <ScalarProperty Name="DesignationID" ParameterName=
"DesignationID" />
          </AssociationEnd>
</DeleteFunction>
<DeleteFunction FunctionName="PayrollModel.Store.ProvidentFund_
Delete">
             <ScalarProperty Name="PFID" ParameterName="PFID" />
             <AssociationEnd AssociationSet="FK_ProvidentFund_
Employee" From="ProvidentFund" To="Employee">
                <ScalarProperty Name="EmployeeID" ParameterName=
"EmployeeID" />
             </AssociationEnd>
</DeleteFunction>
<DeleteFunction FunctionName="PayrollModel.Store.Salary_Delete">
             <ScalarProperty Name="SalaryID"
ParameterName="SalaryID" />
             <AssociationEnd AssociationSet="FK_Salary_Employee"
From="Salary" To="Employee">
                <ScalarProperty Name="EmployeeID" ParameterName=
"EmployeeID" />
             </AssociationEnd>
```

```xml
            <AssociationEnd AssociationSet="FK_Salary_
ProvidentFund" From="Salary" To="ProvidentFund">
                <ScalarProperty Name="PFID" ParameterName="PFID" />
            </AssociationEnd>
</DeleteFunction>
<DeleteFunction FunctionName="PayrollModel.Store.Designation_Delete">
            <ScalarProperty Name="DesignationID" ParameterName=
"DesignationID" />
</DeleteFunction>
<DeleteFunction FunctionName="PayrollModel.Store.Department_Delete">
            <ScalarProperty Name="DepartmentID" ParameterName=
"DepartmentID" />
</DeleteFunction>
```

If you update your model from the database later, you will lose all these customizations. So, you can copy these customizations in a text file and paste them back at the appropriate places if you have updated your model.

Mapping Stored Procedures with No Entity Set

At the time of this writing, the ADO.NET Entity Data Model code generator doesn't include code for functions that return scalar types. That is, Import Functions that don't have any EntitySets. In essence, if your stored procedure returns a single value while not returning an entity or a collection of entities, you will not find code for the function in the generated code. The Stored Procedures that we have used to map to corresponding Function Imports don't have any return type.

You can easily map Stored Procedures that return an existing Entity Type or a collection of Entity Types. To map a Stored Procedure that doesn't return an Entity Type and enable the code generator to generate code for you, just create a dummy table in your database and an Entity Type from that table in the EDM designer. You can now designate this Entity Type as the return type for the function imports in your EDM that doesn't return Entity Types. The other alternative is to use the Entity Client to invoke stored procedures and perform CUD operations though the EDM.

Using Stored Procedures

Let now discuss how we can use the Entity Client to insert Department data. To do this, follow these simple steps:

1. Create an instance of the `EntityConnection` class as shown below:

   ```
   EntityConnection conn = new EntityConnection
                           ("Name=PayrollEntities");
   ```

2. Open the connection using the `EntityConnection` instance:

   ```
   conn.Open();
   ```

3. Create an `EntityCommand` instance and specify the `CommandText` and `CommandType` properties:

   ```
   EntityCommand cmd = conn.CreateCommand();
   cmd.CommandText = "PayrollEntities.InsertDepartment";
   cmd.CommandType = CommandType.StoredProcedure;
   ```

4. Add parameters using the `AddWithValue()` method of the `Parameters` collection of the `EntityCommand` instance:

   ```
   cmd.Parameters.AddWithValue
   ("DepartmentName", "Finance");
   ```

5. Next, execute the procedure using the `ExecuteNonQuery()` method:

   ```
   cmd.ExecuteNonQuery();
   ```

Here is the complete code listing:

```
using (EntityConnection conn = new EntityConnection("Name=
                                                    PayrollEntities"))
{
    try
    {
        conn.Open();
        EntityCommand cmd = conn.CreateCommand();
        cmd.CommandText = "PayrollEntities.InsertDepartment";
        cmd.CommandType = CommandType.StoredProcedure;
        cmd.Parameters.AddWithValue
        ("DepartmentName", "Finance");
        cmd.ExecuteNonQuery();
    }
    catch (Exception ex)
    {
        Response.Write(ex.ToString());
    }
}
```

Mapping Stored Procedures that Return Custom Entity Types

In this section, we will discuss how we can use the EDM to map stored procedures that return miscellaneous data. Let's consider a scenario where we need to create an entity that returns the EmployeeID, FirstName, and LastName of all employees who are no longer working in the organization.

To do this, follow these steps:

1. Create a stored procedure called `OldEmployees`. Here is the script:

   ```
   Create procedure OldEmployees
   as
   Select EmployeeID, FirstName, LastName from Employee where
   LeavingDate is not null
   ```

2. Create an Entity called `OldEmployees` in the EDM with the property names matching the corresponding field names of the stored procedure.

3. Create an `EntityType` called `OldEmployees` in the CSDL

   ```
   <EntityType Name="OldEmployees">
       <Key>
         <PropertyRef Name="EmployeeID" />
       </Key>
         <Property Name="EmployeeID" Type="Int32"
                                     Nullable="false" />
         <Property Name="FirstName" Type="Int32"
                                     Nullable="true" />
         <Property Name="LastName" Type="Int32"
                                     Nullable="true" />
   </EntityType>
   ```

4. Create an `EntitySet` called `OldEmployeesSet` in the CSDL:

   ```
   <EntitySet Name="OldEmployeesSet" EntityType="PayrollModel.OldEmployees" />
   ```

5. Create an `EntityType` called `OldEmployees` in the SSDL:

   ```
   <EntityType Name=" OldEmployees">
       <Key>
         <PropertyRef Name="EmployeeID" />
       </Key>
       <Property Name="EmployeeID" Type="int"
                                   Nullable="false" />
       <Property Name="FirstName" Type="varchar"
                                   Nullable="false" MaxLength="50" />
   ```

```
                <Property Name="LastName" Type="varchar"
                                Nullable="false" MaxLength="50" />
        </EntityType>
```

6. Create an `EntitySet` called `OldEmployeesSet` in the SSDL:

   ```
   <EntitySet Name="OldEmployeesSet" EntityType="PayrollModel.Store.
   OldEmployees" Schema="dbo"/>
   ```

7. Create a Import Function in the CSDL:

   ```
   <FunctionImport Name="GetOldEmployees" EntitySet="OldEmployee"
   ReturnType="Collection(Self.OldEmployees)" />
   ```

8. Now, specify CSDL-MSL mappings in the Mapping layer (MSL) to map the Entity in the Conceptual Layer (CSDL) to the Entity in the Storage Layer (SSDL).

That's it. You are done!

Summary

In this chapter, we have learned how to map stored procedures in the EDM and use them in our applications. We have also discussed how we can map stored procedures that return custom entities. In the next chapter, we will discuss Entity SQL and Entity Client and how we can use them to perform CRUD operations against the EDM.

5
Working with Entity Client and Entity SQL

The ADO.NET Entity Framework contains a powerful client-side query engine that allows you to execute queries against the conceptual model of data, irrespective of the underlying data store in use. This query engine works with a rich functional language called Entity SQL (or E-SQL for short), a derivative of T-SQL, that enables you to query entities or collection of entities.

In this chapter, we will take a look at both Entity Client and Entity SQL, and learn how to use them in our applications.

We will discuss the following areas:

- An overview of the Entity SQL Language
- Differences between Entity SQL and Transact SQL
- When to choose Entity SQL over LINQ
- Working with the Entity Client
- Transaction Management in the Entity Framework

Before we get started with Entity Client, we should have a proper understanding of Entity SQL. This is, the T-SQL like query language used by the Entity Client provider. We will start this chapter with a discussion on the Entity SQL language, and then discuss how we can work with the Entity Client provider.

An Overview of the Entity SQL Language

The Entity Framework allows you to write programs against the Entity Data Model and also, add a level of abstraction on top of the relational model. This isolation of the logical view of data from the Object Model is accomplished by expressing queries in terms of abstractions using an enhanced query language called Entity SQL. This language is specially designed to query data from the Entity Data Model. Entity SQL was designed to address the need for a language that can query data from its conceptual view, rather than its logical view.

From Transact SQL (T-SQL) to Entity SQL (E-SQL)

Standard Query Language or SQL is the primary language that has been in use for years for querying databases. Remember, SQL is a standard and not owned by any particular database vendor. SQL-92 is a standard, and is the most popular SQL standard currently in use. This standard was released in 1992The 92 in the name reflects this fact. Different database vendors have implemented their own flavors of the SQL-92 standard.

The T-SQL language was designed by Microsoft as an SQL Server implementation of the SQL-92 standard. Similar to other SQL languages implemented by different database vendors, the Entity SQL language is the Entity Framework implementation of the SQL-92 standard that can be used to query data from the EDM.

Entity SQL is a text-based, provider independent, late bound query language used by Entity Framework to express queries in terms of EDM abstractions and to query data from the conceptual layer of the Entity Data Model.

One of the major differences between E-SQL and T-SQL is in nested queries. Note that you should always enclose your nested queries in E-SQL using parentheses as seen here:

```
SELECT d, (SELECT DEREF (e) FROM NAVIGATE (d, PayrollEntities.
FK_Employee_Department) AS e) AS Employees FROM PayrollEntities.
Department AS d;
```

The "Select VALUE..." statement is used to retrieve singleton values. It is also used to retrieve values that don't have any column names. However, the "Select ROW..." statement is used to select one or more rows. As an example, if you want a value as a collection from an entity without the column name, you can use the VALUE keyword in the SELECT statement as shown here:

```
SELECT VALUE emp.EmployeeName FROM PayrollEntities.Employee as emp
```

The above statement will return the employee names from the `Employee` entity as a collection of strings.

In T-SQL, you can have the ORDER BY clause at the end of the last query when using UNION ALL.

```
SELECT EmployeeID, EmployeeName
From Employee
UNION ALL
SELECT EmployeeID, Basic, Allowances
FROM Salary
ORDER BY EmployeeID
```

On the contrary, you do not have the ORDER BY clause in the UNION ALL operator in E-SQL.

Why Entity SQL When I Already have LINQ to Entities?

LINQ to Entities is a new version of LINQ, well suited for Entity Framework. But why do you need E-SQL when you already have LINQ to Entities available to you? LINQ to Entities queries are verified at the time of compilation. Therefore, it is not at all suited for building and executing dynamic queries. On the contrary, Entity SQL queries are verified at runtime so they can be used for building and executing dynamic queries. You now have a new ADO.NET Provider in E-SQL, which is a sophisticated query engine that can be used to query your data from the conceptual model. It should be noted, however, that both LINQ and Entity SQL queries are converted into canonical command trees that are in turn translated into database specific query statements based on the underlying database provider in use.

We will now have a quick look at the features of Entity SQL before we delve deep into this language.

Features of Entity SQL

These are the features of Entity SQL:

- *Provider neutrality*: Entity SQL is independent of the underlying ADO.NET Data Provider in use because it works on top of the conceptual model.
- *SQL like*: The syntax of Entity SQL statements resemble T-SQL.

- *Expressive with support for entities and types*: You can write your Entity SQL queries in terms of EDM abstractions.
- *Composable and Orthogonal*: You can use a sub-query wherever you have support for an expression of that type. The sub-queries are all treated uniformly regardless of where they have been used.

In the sections that follow, we will take a look at the Entity SQL language in depth. We will discuss the following points:

- Operators
- Expressions
- Identifiers
- Variables
- Parameters
- Canonical Functions

Operators in Entity SQL

An operator is one that operates on a particular operand to perform an operation. Operators in Entity SQL can broadly be classified into the following categories:

- *Arithmetic Operators*: Perform arithmetic operations.
- *Logical Operators*: Perform logical operations.
- *Comparison Operators*: You can use to compare the values of two operands.
- *Reference Operators*: Act as logical pointers to a particular entity belonging to a particular entity set.
- *Type Operators*: Can operate on the type of an expression.
- *Case Operators*: Operate on a set of boolean expressions.
- *Set Operators*: Operate on set operations.

Arithmetic Operators

Here is an example of an arithmetic operator:

```
SELECT VALUE s FROM PayrollEntities.Salary AS s
    where s.Basic = 5000 + 1000
```

The following arithmetic operators available in Entity SQL:

- + (Add)
- - (Subtract)
- / (Divide)
- % (Modulo)
- * (Multiply)

Comparison Operators

Here is an example of a comparison operator:

```
SELECT VALUE e FROM PayrollEntities.Employee
    AS e where e.EmployeeID = 1
```

Below is a list of the comparison operators available in Entity SQL:

- = (Equals)
- != (Not equal to)
- <> (Not equal to)
- > (Greater than)
- < (Less than)
- >= (Greater than or equal to)
- <= (Less than or equal to)
- [NOT] Like
- [NOT] Between

Logical Operators

Here is an example of using logical operators in Entity SQL:

```
SELECT VALUE s FROM PayrollEntities.Salary
    AS s where s.Basic > 5000 && s.Allowances > 3000
```

Here is a list of the logical operators available in Entity SQL:

- && (And)
- ! (Not)
- || (Or)

Reference Operators

The following is an example of how you can use a reference operator in Entity SQL:

```
SELECT VALUE REF(e).FirstName FROM PayrollEntities.Employee
 as e
```

The following is a list of the reference operators available in Entity SQL:

- Key
- Ref
- CreateRef
- DeRef

Type Operators

Here is an example of a type operator that returns a collection of employees from a collection of persons:

```
SELECT VALUE e FROM
     OFTYPE(PayrollEntities.Person, PayrollEntities.Employee) AS e
```

The following is a list of the type operators available in Entity SQL:

- OfType
- Cast
- Is [Not] Of
- Treat

Set Operators

Here is an example of how you can use a set operator in Entity SQL:

```
(Select VALUE e from PayrollEntities.Employee
    as e where e.FirstName Like 'J%') Union All
    ( select VALUE s from PayrollEntities.Employee
    as s where s.DepartmentID = 1)
```

Here is a list of the set operators available in Entity SQL:

- Set
- Union
- Element
- AnyElement

- Except
- [Not] Exists
- [Not] In
- Overlaps
- Intersect

Operator Precedence

When you have multiple operators operating in a sequence, the order in which the operators will be executed will be determined by the operator precedence. The following table shows the operator, operator type, and their precedence levels in Entity SQL language:

Operators	Operator Type	Precedence Level
., [] ()	Primary	Level 1
! not	Unary	Level 2
* / %	Multiplicative	Level 3
+ and -	Additive	Level 4
< > <= >=	Relational	Level 5
= != <>	Equality	Level 6
and &&	Conditional And	Level 7
or ||	Conditional Or	Level 8

Expressions in Entity SQL

Expressions are the building blocks of the Entity SQL language. Here are some examples of how expressions are represented:

```
1;        //This represents one scalar item
{2};      //This represents a collection of one element
{3, 4, 5} //This represents a collection of multiple elements
```

Query Expressions in Entity SQL

Query expressions are used in conjunction with query operators to perform a certain operation and return a result set. Query expressions in Entity SQL are actually a series of clauses that are represented using one or more of the following:

- SELECT: This clause is used to specify or limit the number of elements that are returned when a query is executed in Entity SQL.
- FROM: This clause is used to specify the source or collection for retrieval of the elements in a query.

- **WHERE:** This clause is used to specify a particular expression.
- **HAVING:** This clause is used to specify a filter condition for retrieval of the result set.
- **GROUP BY:** This clause is used to group the elements returned by a query.
- **ORDER BY:** This clause is used to order the elements returned in either ascending or descending order.

Here is the complete syntax of query expressions in Entity SQL:

```
SELECT VALUE [ ALL | DISTINCT ] FROM expression [ ,...n ] as C [ WHERE
expression ]
[ GROUP BY expression [ ,...n ] ] [ HAVING search_condition ] [ ORDER
BY expression]
```

And here is an example of a typical Entity SQL query with all clause types being used:

```
SELECT emp.FirstName FROM PayrollEntities.Employee emp,
PayrollEntities.Department dept Group By dept.DepartmentName Where
emp.DepartmentID = dept.DepartmentID Having emp.EmployeeID > 5
```

Identifiers, Variables, Parameters, and Types in Entity SQL

Identifiers in Entity SQL are of the following two types:

- Simple Identifiers
- Quoted Identifiers

Simple Identifiers are a sequence of alphanumeric or underscore characters. Note that an identifier should always begin with an alphabetical character.

As an example, the following are valid identifiers:

```
a12_ab
M_09cd
W0001m
```

However, the following are invalid identifiers:

```
9abcd
_xyz
0_pqr
```

Quoted identifiers are those that are enclosed within square brackets ([]). Here are some examples of quoted identifiers:

```
SELECT emp.EmployeeName AS [Employee Name] FROM Employee as emp
SELECT dept.DepartmentName AS [Department Name] FROM Department as
dept
```

Chapter 5

> Quoted identifiers cannot contain new line, tab, backspace or carriage return characters.

In Entity SQL, a variable is a reference to a named expression. Note that the naming conventions for variables follow the same rules for an identifier. In other words, a valid variable reference to a named expression in Entity SQL should be a valid identifier too. Here is an example:

```
SELECT emp FROM Employee as emp;
```

In the above example, `emp` is a variable reference. Types can be of three versions:

- Primitive types like integers and strings.
- Nominal types such as entity types, entity sets, and relationships.
- Transient types like rows, collections, and references.

The Entity SQL language supports the following type categories:

- Rows
- Collections
- References

Row

A row, which is also known as a tuple, has no identity or behaviour and cannot be inherited.

The following statement returns one row that contains six elements:

```
ROW (1, 'Joydip');
```

Collection

Collections represent zero or more instances of other instances.

You can use `SET ()` to retrieve unique values from a collection of values. Here is an example:

```
SET({1,1,2,2,3,3,4,4,5,5,6,6})
```

The above will return the unique values from the set. Specifically, `2, 3, 4, 5, and 6`.

[111]

This is equivalent to the following statement:

```
Select Value Distinct x from {1,1,2,2,3,3,4,4,5,5,6,6} As x;
```

You can create collections using `MULTISET ()` or even using `{}` as shown in the following examples:

```
MULTISET (1, 2, 3, 4, 5, 6)
```

The following represents the same as above:

```
{1, 2, 3, 4, 5, 6}
```

Here is how you can return a collection of ten identical rows each with six elements in them:

```
SELECT ROW(1,'Joydip') from {1,2,3,4,5,6,7,8,9,10}
```

To return a collection of all rows from the employee set, you can use the following:

```
Select emp from PayrollEntities.Employee as emp;
```

Similarly, to select all rows from the department set, you use the following:

```
Select dept from PayrollEntities.Department as dept;
```

Reference

A reference denotes a logical pointer, or reference, to a particular entity. In essence, it is a foreign key to a specific entity set.

Operators are used to perform operations on one or more operands. In Entity SQL, the following operators are available to construct, deconstruct, and also navigate through references:

- KEY
- REF
- CREATEREF
- DEREF

> To create a reference to an instance of Employee, you can use REF() as shown here:
> ```
> SELECT REF (emp) FROM PayrollEntities.Employee as emp
> ```
> Once you have created a reference to an entity using REF(), you can also dereference the entity using DREF() as shown below:
> ```
> DEREF (CREATEREF(PayrollEntities.Employee, ROW(@
> EmployeeID)))
> ```

Canonical Functions in Entity SQL

Entity SQL supports a wide variety of canonical functions. These can broadly be classified into the following categories:

- *Mathematical*: These are used to perform calculations based on some numeric values.
- *Aggregate*: These are used to perform calculations based on a set of input values.
- *Bitwise*: These are used to perform bitwise operations.
- *String*: These are used to perform string operations.
- *Date and Time*: These are used to perform operations on date time values. For example, SystemDateTime values.

Mathematical Functions

Here is a list of the mathematical canonical functions available in Entity SQL:

- `Floor` (value): Returns the largest integer that is not greater than the value passed to it as argument.
- `Abs` (value): Returns the absolute value of the value passed to it as argument.
- `Ceiling` (value): Returns the smallest integer that is not less than the value passed to it as argument.
- `Round` (value): Returns a rounded integer value, rounded to the nearest integer, for the value passed to it as argument.

Aggregate Functions

The following is a list of the aggregate canonical functions available in Entity SQL:

- `Avg` (expression): Returns the average of the values passed.
- `Max` (expression): Returns the maximum value of the values passed to it as argument.
- `Min` (expression): Returns the minimum value of the values passed.
- `Count` (expression): Returns a count of the values passed.
- `Sum` (expression): Returns the sum of the values passed as an expression.

The following statement makes use of aggregate canonical functions to return the minimum, average, and maximum of the basic salary for employees from the Salary table.

```
SELECT MIN(s.Basic), AVG(s.Basic), MAX(s.Basic) FROM PayrollEntities.
Salary as s
```

String Functions

Here is a list of the string canonical functions available:

- `Length` (string): Returns the length of the string passed to it as an argument.
- `Concat` (string1, string2): Appends the second string to the first and returns a new string.
- `IndexOf` (string1, string2): Returns the index or position of the first string in the second.
- `Left` (string1, length): Returns the number of characters specified by length from the left of the string instance represented by string1.
- `Trim` (string1): Trims the leading and trailing spaces from the string instance passed to it as argument.
- `LTrim` (string1): Trims the leading spaces only from the string instance.
- `RTrim` (string1): Trims the trailing spaces only from the string instance.
- `Substring` (string1, start position, length): Returns a sub string from the string instance beginning with the start position and represented by the number of characters specified by length.
- `Reverse` (string1): Reverses the string instance passed to it as argument.
- `Replace` (string1, string2, string3): Replaces all occurrences of string2 with string3 in the instance string1.

Bitwise Functions

The following is a list of the Bitwise canonical functions available in Entity SQL:

- `BitwiseAnd` (value1, value2): Performs a bitwise 'and' operation between value1 and value2.
- `BitwiseOr` (value1, value2): Performs a bitwise 'or' operation between value1 and value2.
- `BitwiseNot` (value): Performs a bitwise 'not' operation with the value passed to it as argument.
- `BitwiseXor` (value1, value2): Performs a bitwise 'xor' operation between value1 and value2.

Date and Time Functions

Here is the list of the available Date and Time canonical functions:

- `GetDate()`: Gets the current system date time value.
- `Second` (datetime): Returns the second portion of the current system date time value.
- `Minute` (datetime): Returns the minute portion of the current system date time value.
- `Hour` (datetime): Returns the hour portion of the current system date time value.
- `Day` (datetime): Returns the day portion of the current system date.
- `Month` (datetime): Returns the month portion of the current system date.
- `Year` (datetime): Returns the year portion of the current system date.

Data Paging Using Entity SQL

Data paging is a concept that allows you to retrieve a specified number of records and display them in the user interface. The data is displayed one page at a time. You can use data paging to split the data rendered to the user into multiple pages for faster page downloads, an increase to user interface flexibility, and minimal load on the database server. Paging can be used when the volume of data to be displayed is substantial and you need it to be divided into pages of data records to be displayed more efficiently.

The following statement will return a result set that contains the top 10 records of the `Employee` table, ordered by employee names:

```
SELECT emp FROM PayrollEntities.Employee AS emp ORDER BY emp.
EmployeeName LIMIT 10;
```

Suppose you need to display records 11 to 20 from the `Employee` table. Here is how you can do this:

```
SELECT emp FROM PayrollEntities.Employee AS emp ORDER BY emp.
EmployeeName SKIP 10 LIMIT 10;
```

How does it work? When you say `SKIP 10`, it will skip 10 records while the `LIMIT` clause limits the retrieval to 10 records only. Therefore, you end up with records 11 to 20 from the `Employee` table.

> LINQ to SQL also has `SKIP` and `TAKE`. It is important to know that this is database paging where only the relevant rows are returned versus the default paging of standard ASP.NET data controls.

Working with the ADO.NET Entity Client

The ADO.NET Entity Client is a data provider that provides a gateway for executing entity level queries using the Entity Framework. You can use it to query against your conceptual model of data. Entity Client uses its own language called Entity SQL, a storage independent language, to communicate with the conceptual model. You can execute the same Entity SQL query against any data store. In other words it is provider independent and you need not make changes to your query if the underlying data store changes. Therefore, you can use the same Entity SQL syntax to talk to the conceptual model, regardless of the data store in use.

The Entity SQL queries are converted to a command tree that is in turn passed to the storage specific provider to generate native SQL statements. As an example, if you are using SQL Server as the database, the Entity SQL queries that you are using will be converted to a command tree that will be passed to the ADO.NET provider for SQL Server. This allows the ADO.NET provider to generate statements specific to SQL Server database.

Similar to the ADO.NET provider, the Entity Client provider follows the pattern of Connection, Command, or DataReader, and so forth. The class names are all prefixed with "Entity". Therefore, you have classes like, EntityConnection that represents a connection, EntityCommand that represents a command, EntityDataReader that represents a data reader, and so on.

In this section, we will take a look at how we can use the ADO.NET Entity Client to execute queries against the Entity Data Model. The System.Data.EntityClient namespace represents the ADO.NET Entity Client Provider. That is, a standard ADO.NET managed provider that we will use to access a database and execute queries or perform inserts, updates, and deletes. To just let you know the resemblance between Entity Client data provider and ADO.NET data provider, here are two samples:

First, here is how you use the ADO.NET data provider to connect to a database and display records from its table:

```
using (SQLConnection sqlConnection = new SQLConnection(connectionStri
ng))
{
    sqlConnection.Open();
    String queryString = "Select * from Employee";
    SQLCommand sqlCommand = new SQLCommand(queryString,
sqlConnection);
    SQLDataReader dataReader = sqlCommand.ExecuteReader(CommandBehavio
r.SequentialAccess);
      while (dataReader.Read())
```

```
    {
        Console.WriteLine(dataReader.GetValue(0));
    }
}
```

Second, here is the EntitySQL counterpart of what was just demonstrated:

```
using (EntityConnection entityConnection = new EntityConnection(conne
ctionString))
{
    entityConnection.Open();
    String queryString = "Select value e from PayrollEntities.Employee 
as e";
    using (EntityCommand entityCommand = new EntityCommand(queryString
, entityConnection))
    {
        using (DbDataReader dataReader = entityCommand.ExecuteReader(C
ommandBehavior.SequentialAccess))
        {
            while (dataReader.Read())
            {
                Console.WriteLine(dataReader.GetValue(0));
            }
        }
    }
}
```

Let's Get into Action

The following is a sequence of steps you can follow to work with the Entity Client:

1. Building a connection string
2. Creating an Entity Connection
3. Opening the connection
4. Executing queries using Entity Command
5. Closing the connection

Building the Connection String

You can use the `EntityConnectionStringBuilder` class to create your database connection string and use it to connect to the database. This section discusses how this is accomplished.

To build a connection for use with the EntityClient, follow these steps:

1. Create an instance of the `SqlConnectionStringBuilder` class and specify the data source, database name, database server to connect to, user id, and password.

   ```
   SqlConnectionStringBuilder sqlConnectionStringBuilder = new
   SqlConnectionStringBuilder();
   sqlConnectionStringBuilder.DataSource = ".";
   sqlConnectionStringBuilder.InitialCatalog = "test";
   sqlConnectionStringBuilder.IntegratedSecurity = false;
   sqlConnectionStringBuilder.UserID = "sa";
   sqlConnectionStringBuilder.Password = "sa";
   ```

2. Now, create an instance of the `EntityConnectionStringBuilder` class and specify the metadata location, the provider name, and the provider connection string.

   ```
   EntityConnectionStringBuilder entityConnectionStringBuilder =
   new EntityConnectionStringBuilder();
   entityConnectionStringBuilder.Metadata = ".";
   entityConnectionStringBuilder.Provider = "System.Data.SqlClient";
   entityConnectionStringBuilder.ProviderConnectionString =
   sqlConnectionStringBuilder.ToString();
   entityConnectionStringBuilder.Metadata = ".";
   ```

Creating an Entity Connection

Now that we have built our entity connection string, we will now create a entity connection instance and open the connection.

You need to create the entity connection instance using the `EntityConnection` class and pass the connection string we just created to the constructor. Here is how it is done:

```
EntityConnection entityConnection =
    new EntityConnection(entityConnectionStringBuilder.ToString());
```

Opening the Connection

To open the connection, you need to invoke the `Open()` method on the entity connection instance as shown here:

```
entityConnection.Open();
```

Before we move ahead, we should test the connection to verify whether the connection was opened successfully. Here is how you can do this:

```
using (EntityConnection entityConnection =
    new EntityConnection(entityConnectionStringBuilder.ToString()))
{
    entityConnection.Open();
    if(entityConnection.State == ConnectionState.Open)
    Console.WriteLine("Connection opened successfully.");
}
```

Note the use of the keyword using. When you execute the above snippet, the message **Connection opened successfully** will be displayed. Once you have opened the connection, you can begin executing your queries using Entity SQL.

Executing Queries Using the Entity Command

Let's use an example to help us understand how you can make use of Entity SQL to leverage the power of Entity Data Model. Suppose you need to display the names and contact details of all the employees who are working in the HR department. Here is how you can do this using T-SQL:

```
SELECT Employee.FirstName, Employee.LastName, Contact.Address,
Contact.PhoneNo FROM Employee, Contacts, Department
INNER JOIN
    Contacts ON Employee.ContactID = Contact.ContactID
INNER JOIN
    Department ON Employee.DepartmentID = Department.DepartmentID
WHERE Department.DepartmentName = "HR"
```

If you use Entity SQL, the query can become much simpler:

```
SELECT FirstName, LastName, Address, PhoneNo FROM HREmployees
```

No joins! Yes, now you can do without joins. You simply need to inherit a new entity called HRemployees from Employee, Contacts, and Department entities. Note that the fields FirstName, LastName, Address, and PhoneNo will be the properties of this new derived entity. We just changed from the database schema specific T-SQL to a more abstract E-SQL that queries against a conceptual model of our data rather than a logical model as in the former case.

What we require now is an entity command instance to execute the query. Here is how you can do this:

```
String sqlString = "SELECT FirstName, LastName, Address, PhoneNo FROM HREmployees";
EntityCommand entityCommand = new EntityCommand (sqlString, entityConnection);
```

So, what did we just do? We created an entity command instance and passed the query string and the entity connection instance to its constructor as parameters.

Now that our entity command instance is in place, we can execute the query as shown below:

```
EntityDataReader entityDataReader = entityCommand.ExecuteReader (CommandBehavior.SequentialAccess);
```

Refer to the code snippet above. We called the ExecuteReader() method on the entity command instance to execute the query. This method will execute the query and return a result set as an entity data reader instance.

To iterate through the records, we need to call the Read() method on the entity data reader instance as shown here:

```
while (reader.Read())
{

}
```

We will now iterate this instance and display the records as shown below:

```
while (reader.Read())
  Response.Write(reader[0].ToString()+"\t"+
  reader[1].ToString());
```

Adding Properties that Do Not Have a Corresponding Database Mapping

Note that you cannot add a property in the model unless it has a corresponding database mapping. You can, however, overcome this limitation by using partial classes. Here is how you can add a new property called PFACCNo (that doesn't have a corresponding mapping in the database) in the Employee entity:

```
namespace PayrollModel
{
  public partial class Employee
  {
      private int pfAccNo;
      public int PFACCNo
      {
        get
        {
          return pfAccNo;
        }
        set
        {
          m_value = pfAccNo;
        }
      }
  }
}
```

Executing Nested Queries in Entity SQL

Here is how nested queries are used in Entity SQL.

The following statement returns a collection of rows where each row contains a department entity and its reference to the corresponding employee entity:

```
SELECT d, (SELECT DEREF (e) FROM NAVIGATE (d,
PayrollEntities.FK_Employee_Department) AS e) AS
Employees FROM PayrollEntities.Department AS d;
```

Closing the Connection

If you are done using the entity connection instance, you should close your connection by invoking the Close() method on your entity connection instance. Here is how you will do this:

```
entityConnection.Close();
```

You can also check whether the connection is open prior to closing using the `ConnectionState` enum int as shown here:

```
if(entityConnection.State == ConnectionState.Open)
        entityConnection.Close();
```

And, here is the complete source code of what we just did:

```
SqlConnectionStringBuilder sqlConnectionStringBuilder =   new
SqlConnectionStringBuilder();
sqlConnectionStringBuilder.DataSource = ".";
sqlConnectionStringBuilder.InitialCatalog = "test";
sqlConnectionStringBuilder.IntegratedSecurity = false;
sqlConnectionStringBuilder.UserID = "sa";
sqlConnectionStringBuilder.Password = "sa";

EntityConnectionStringBuilder entityConnectionStringBuilder =
new EntityConnectionStringBuilder();
entityConnectionStringBuilder.Metadata = ".";
entityConnectionStringBuilder.Provider = "System.Data.SqlClient";
entityConnectionStringBuilder.ProviderConnectionString =
sqlConnectionStringBuilder.ToString();
entityConnectionStringBuilder.Metadata = ".";
using (EntityConnection entityConnection =
    new EntityConnection(entityConnectionStringBuilder.ToString()))
{
   entityConnection.Open();
   String sqlString = "SELECT FirstName, LastName, Address, PhoneNo
FROM HREmployees";
   EntityCommand entityCommand = new EntityCommand (sqlString,
entityConnection);
   EntityDataReader entityDataReader = entityCommand.ExecuteReader
(CommandBehavior.SequentialAccess);

  while (reader.Read())
    Response.Write(reader[0].ToString()+"\t"+
    reader[1].ToString());

    if(entityConnection.State == ConnectionState.Open)
        entityConnection.Close();
}
```

Other Operations with Entity SQL

In this section, we will take a look at how we can perform some additional operations with the Entity SQL language. We will discuss the following:

- Inserting a record using Entity SQL
- Inserting a record with a foreign key constraint
- Retrieving native SQL from EntityCommand
- Transaction Management in Entity SQL

Inserting a Record Using Entity SQL

You can use Entity SQL statements and easily perform CRUD operations. Let's assume that you have a stored procedure called InsertDesignation and you would like to use it to store a record in the designation table of your Payroll database. Here is the code:

```
using (EntityConnection conn = new EntityConnection("Name=PayrollEnti
ties"))
 {
 try
  {
     conn.Open();
     EntityCommand cmd = conn.CreateCommand();
   cmd.CommandText = "PayrollEntities.Employee_Insert";
   cmd.CommandType = CommandType.StoredProcedure;
   cmd.Parameters.AddWithValue("FirstName", "Joydip");
   cmd.Parameters.AddWithValue("LastName", "Kanjilal");
   cmd.Parameters.AddWithValue("Address", "Kolkata");
   cmd.Parameters.AddWithValue("Phone", "123456789");
   cmd.Parameters.AddWithValue("JoiningDate", DateTime.Now);
   cmd.Parameters.AddWithValue("LeavingDate", null);
   cmd.Parameters.AddWithValue("DepartmentID", 2);
   cmd.Parameters.AddWithValue("DesignationID", 1);
 cmd.ExecuteNonQuery();
  }
 catch (Exception ex)
  {
    Response.Write(ex.ToString());
  }
 }
```

Inserting a Record with a Foreign Key Constraint

Here is an example that shows how you can insert a single row that has a foreign key constraint without doing an extra select:

```
Employee employee = new Employee();
employee.EmployeeID = 25;
employee.EmployeeName = "Rituraj";
employee.DepartmentMasterReference = new System.Data.Objects.
DataClasses.EntityReference<Department>();
employee.DepartmentMasterReference = new EntityKey("PayrollEntities.
Department", "DepartmentID", "3");
```

Retrieving Native SQL from EntityCommand

You can retrieve native SQL from an EntityCommand instance by using the `ToTraceString()` method on the EntityCommand instance. Here is an example:

```
using (EntityConnection entityConnection = new EntityConnection
(ConnectionString))
{
  String sqlString = "SELECT VALUE emp from PayrollEntities.Employee as emp";
             EntityCommand entityCommand = entityConnection.
CreateCommand();
             entityCommand.CommandText = sqlString;
             entityConnection.Open();
             // Displaying the Entity SQL text using the
CommandText property
             Console.WriteLine(entityCommand.CommandText);
             // Display the T-SQL text using the ToTraceString()
method.
             Console.WriteLine(entityCommand.ToTraceString());
    //Other code

    entityConnection.Close();
}
```

Transaction Management in Entity SQL

A transaction is a group of statements that are guaranteed to be executed in their entirety. If any statements inside a transaction fail, the entire transaction is rolled back. In other words, any changes to the database are rolled back, if changes were indeed made. You can use transactions in two ways in the Entity Framework. Namely, using either the EntityTransaction class or the System.Transactions namespace. EntityTransaction is an enhanced version of System.Data.Common. DbTransaction with better support for transaction commit and rollbacks. However, you can't create an instance of EntityTransaction as its constructor is internal.

Here is an example of how you can use the EntityTransaction class for transaction management in the Entity Framework:

```
using(EntityConnection entityConnection = new EntityConnection
(connectionString))
{
  entityConnection.Open();
  EntityTransaction entityTransaction = entityConnection.
BeginTransaction(IsolationLevel.Snapshot);
  EntityCommand entityCommand1 = entityConnection.CreateCommand();
  entityCommand1.CommandText = "SELECT VALUE e FROM PayrollEntities.
Employee AS e";
  entityCommand1.Transaction = entityTransaction;
  EntityDataReader entityDataReader1 = entityCommand.ExecuteReader();
   while(entityDataReader1.Read())
   {
     //Some code
     EntityCommand entityCommand2 = con.CreateCommand();
     entityCommand2.CommandText =
            "SELECT Value s from PayrollEntities.Sales as s Where
s.EmployeeID = @EmployeeID";
     entityCommand2.Transaction = entityTransaction;
     DbDataReader dataReader = entityCommand2.ExecuteReader();
     // Do some processing here
   }
  entityTransaction.Commit();
}
```

It should be noted that when you call the BeginTransaction() method on the connection instance, it starts an explicit transaction on that instance. However, if you want to perform a number of operations on different databases within a single transaction, you can use a transaction scope. In other words, if you are using multiple connection instances belonging to different databases, then, using a transaction scope is a better choice.

You can start a transaction scope by creating an instance of the `TransactionScope` class as shown below:

```
TransactionScope transactionScope = new TransactionScope();
```

Here is an example that illustrates how you can use `TransactionScope` in your applications:

```
EntityConnection entityConnection = new EntityConnection
(ConnectionString);
using (TransactionScope transactionScope = new TransactionScope())
        {
                using (PayrollEntities payrollEntities = new
PayrollEntities(entityConnection))
                {
                        var query = payrollEntities.CreateQuery
<Employee>("Select value e from Employee as e");
                        foreach (Employee emp in query)
                        {
                            Console.WriteLine(emp.FirstName);
                        }
                }
                using (PayrollEntities payrollEntities = new
PayrollEntities(entityConnection))
                {
                        var query = payrollEntities.CreateQuery
<Department>("Select value d from Department as d");
                        foreach (Department dept in query)
                        {
                            Console.WriteLine(dept.DepartmentName);
                        }
                }
                ts.Complete();
        }
```

Summary

In this chapter, we have learned about Entity SQL and how it can be used with the Entity Client provider to perform CRUD operations in our applications. We discussed the differences between Entity SQL and T-SQL and the differences between Entity SQL and LINQ. We also discussed when one should choose Entity SQL instead of LINQ to query data in applications. In the next chapter, we will take a look at Object Services and discuss how it works to perform CRUD operations against the Entity Data Model.

6
Working with LINQ to Entities

LINQ, or Language Integrated Query as it is called, is a query translation pipeline that has been introduced as part of the C# 3.0 library. It is an extension to the C# language and provides a simplified framework for accessing relational data in a strongly typed and object oriented way. You can even use LINQ to query data from other data sources such as XML, objects, and collections.

In this chapter, we will discuss **LINQ to Entities**. We will learn how to use LINQ on top of the Entity Framework and how LINQ can be used to query data against the **Entity Data Model**. We will start our discussion with a quick look at what LINQ is and examine some of its features.

In this chapter, we will learn about the following:

- Introducing LINQ;
- Benefits and Features of LINQ
- Components of the LINQ Architecture
- Understanding LINQ to Entities
- Operators in LINQ
- Expressions in LINQ

Introducing LINQ

Microsoft states, "The LINQ Project is a codename for a set of extensions to the .NET Framework that encompasses language-integrated query, set, and transform operations. It extends C# and Visual Basic with native language syntax for queries and provides class libraries to take advantage of these capabilities." LINQ can be used to map your business objects and the underlying data sources. These data sources can be databases, objects, collections of objects, or even XML document files. Note that both C# 3.0 and VB 9 have support for LINQ. You can find more information about this from the LINQ FAQ at the MSDN forums.

LINQ is a part of the new versions of the **C#** and **VB.NET** compilers and it comes with a powerful set of operators to ease the task of querying different data sources, like SQL Server, XML, and so on. LINQ comprises a standard set of operators to facilitate query operations. We will learn more about LINQ query operators later in this chapter.

Why LINQ?

We often require querying data and displaying them in the presentation layer of our applications. Before LINQ, we used PL-SQL and T-SQL queries to query data from data sources. The major problem with such queries is that there are no compile time checks. With LINQ, you now can do a compile time check and use your type safe queries to query data not only from databases, but also from XML data sources, objects, and collections of objects.

LINQ is a useful new feature available as part of C# 3.0. It allows you to integrate queries directly into your programs. It is an extension to the C# language and provides a simplified framework for accessing relational data in a strongly typed and object oriented manner. Here is how you can search for an employee from our employee table using LINQ:

```
var result =
    from emp in Employee
    where emp.FirstName == "Jini"
    select c.EmployeeID;
```

The above query will return the employee id whose name starts with `Jini`.

Apart from being type safe and having the ability to check queries at compile time, you can easily debug your LINQ queries comfortably, which is a very important feature indeed.

Understanding the LINQ Architecture

A query language is one that is used to query data in our applications. Before LINQ arrived, we used PL-SQL and T-SQL to query data from databases. However, none of them are type safe and don't have compile time checks to verify whether the statements are correct at compile time. In LINQ, we have compile time checks and type safety. Your queries will be verified for accuracy at the compile time itself!

In this section, we will discuss the basic components of the architecture of LINQ. We will now familiarize ourselves with LINQ fundamentals, the components involved in its architecture, and so on. The following figure illustrates the LINQ architecture:

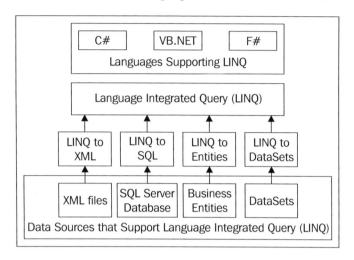

LINQ to XML

LINQ to XML maps your LINQ queries, or LINQ statements, to the corresponding XML data sources. It allows you to use the LINQ standard query operators to retrieve XML data. LINQ to XML is commonly known as **XLINQ**. You can also use LINQ to query your in-memory collections and business entities, objects that contain data related to a particular entity, seamlessly.

LINQ to SQL

Similar to XLINQ, you also have **DLINQ** which is an implementation of LINQ which allows you to query your databases. LINQ to SQL, or DLINQ as it is called, is actually a very simple ORM tool. It is not a complete ORM tool because it lacks some of the features that an ORM has. For example, it doesn't support state management and data generations.

Think of a typical SQL query like this:

    SELECT * from Salary Where Basic > 5000

Here is how you can write the same query using LINQ:

    var query = from s in Salary where s.Basic > 5000 select s;

When using LINQ to SQL, the `DataContext` class in the `System.Data.Linq` namespace is used to create your data contexts. All of your data context classes will derive from the base `DataContext` class. `DataContexts` are responsible for generating the corresponding SQL statements when using LINQ to SQL. In other words, the `DataContext` accepts the LINQ statements as input, processes them, and produces the corresponding **T-SQL** statements as output.

 To use LINQ in your programs, you must add a reference to `System.Core.dll` and specify the System.Linq namespace in the using statement.

LINQ to Objects

LINQ to Objects is another flavor of LINQ that is used to query in memory objects or collections of objects. Note that LINQ to Objects works with `T:System.Collections.IEnumerable` or `T:System.Collections.Generic` in memory objects or collections of objects. Here is an example of a typical LINQ to Objects query that displays the numbers 1 to 9:

```
var myCollection = new[] { 1, 2, 3, 4, 5, 6, 7, 8, 9 };
var data = from d in myCollection
           select d
foreach (var i in d)
Console.WriteLine(i);
```

Let's look at another example that illustrates how you can use LINQ to query a collection of objects. Consider a class `Employee` with three properties as shown below:

```
class Employee
    {
        public string FirstName { get; set; }
        public string LastName { get; set; }
        public string Address { get; set; }
    }
```

Now, you can use LINQ to Objects to query instances of `Employee` as shown below:

```
var employees = new List<Employee> { new Employee
           { FirstName = "Joydip", LastName = "Kanjilal",Address = "Hyderabad" },
           new Employee { FirstName = "Douglas", LastName = "Paterson",Address =  "Birmingham"},
           new Employee { FirstName = "Oindrilla", LastName = "RoyChowdhury", Address = "Kolkata" }
```

```
    };
    var query =
        from employee in employees
        orderby employee.FirstName
        select employee;
```

LINQ to Entities

LINQ, as we already know, defines a set of operators, such as query operators and projection operations, that enables you to query data, traverse data, and express the query and projection operations declaratively in any programming language that targets the Microsoft .NET Framework.

LINQ to Entities enables you to query your business objects from within the language in a strongly typed manner. You can use it to query business objects or collections of business objects from the conceptual data model like the Entity Data Model. LINQ to Entities uses Object Services to query data from the Entity Data Model. Object Services can be used to query data from almost any data store with less code. Apart from enabling you to perform CRUD operations, the Object Services layer provides many additional services like change tracking, lazy loading, and support for querying data using Entity SQL and LINQ to Entities. Note that the Object Services Layer internally uses an Object Query object for query processing. We will take a detailed look at Object Services in the next chapter.

Querying Data Using LINQ to Entities

Here is an example of a typical LINQ to Entities query that returns all department names from the Department table of the Payroll database:

```
PayrollModel.PayrollEntities ctx = new PayrollModel.PayrollEntities();
    var query = from dept in ctx.Department
        select dept;
    foreach (var department in query)
        Response.Write("<BR>"+department.DepartmentName);
```

LINQ to Entities and Entity Framework

Where does LINQ to Entities fit in exactly? You can use LINQ to entities to query the Entity Data Model to retrieve entities or collections of entities. In essence, LINQ to Entities provides you strongly typed access to data that is exposed by the ADO. NET Entity Data Model. In other words, LINQ to Entities enables you to write your queries against a conceptual model of data. LINQ to Entities enables you to create and execute strongly typed and compose-able queries against the Entity Data Model to retrieve entities or collections of entities.

LINQ to Entities uses the Object Services infrastructure to query data from the conceptual model. The `ObjectContext` and `ObjectQuery` classes are two of the most important classes that you use when working with LINQ to Entities. The `ObjectContext` class is used to compose an `ObjectQuery` instance. The generic `ObjectQuery` class represents an entity or a collection of typed entity instances. It should be noted that LINQ to Entities queries are internally translated to canonical query trees. They are then converted internally to corresponding SQL queries in a form expected by your underlying database.

Here is how LINQ to Entities and the ADO.NET Entity Framework are related to each other.

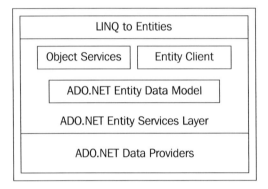

Differences between LINQ to Entities and LINQ to SQL

LINQ to Entities is a super set of LINQ to SQL. The primary use of LINQ to Entities is in defining a domain model for the application and using it for persisting data in the underlying data store that the application uses. LINQ to SQL on the other hand is ideal for two-tiered, three-tiered, or even n-tiered applications.

It should be noted that Microsoft initially had plans to provide support for multiple databases in LINQ to SQL. However, Microsoft has lost interest in the development of LINQ to SQL. Microsoft is more interested in the development of Entity Framework primarily because it has numerous powerful features like entity-splitting, support for table per class, and table per type inheritance models, and it can also support multiple databases.

Two of the major areas where LINQ to Entities is superior to LINQ to SQL are Entity Inheritance and Entity Composition. Using LINQ to Entities, you can create new entities by inheriting existing ones, and, even create entities that are composed of properties of one or more entities.

 Both LINQ to SQL and LINQ to Entities support default inheritance models. That is, you can use both of them to inherit new entities from existing ones.

So which one should I choose and when should I choose it? Generally, ADO.NET Entity Framework and LINQ to Entities is a good choice over LINQ to SQL (formerly DLINQ) if you want your application's code to be loosely coupled and isolated from the changes that may occur in the relational or logical schema of data. It is also a good choice if you want to inherit or compose entities. These features are otherwise not provided by default with LINQ to SQL.

Operators in LINQ

Operators are those that operate on operands to perform a certain task. Powered by a rich set of query operators and expressions, you can use LINQ with absolutely any data such as relational databases and XML files. Moreover, LINQ is type safe and extensible.

LINQ offers a collection of powerful operators that make the task of querying data much easier. The operators in LINQ can be grouped into the following categories, with each category containing one or more operators:

- Aggregation
    - Aggregate
    - Average
    - Count
    - LongCount
    - Min
    - Max
    - Sum
- Concatenation
    - Concat

- Conversion
    - Cast
    - OfType
    - ToArray
    - ToDictionary
    - ToList
    - ToLookup
    - ToSequence
- Element
    - DefaultIfEmpty
    - ElementAt
    - ElementAtOrDefault
    - First
    - FirstOrDefault
    - Last
    - LastOrDefault
    - Single
    - SingleOrDefault
- Equality
    - SequenceEqual
- Generation
    - Empty
    - Range
    - Repeat
- Grouping
    - GroupBy
- Joining
    - GroupJoin
    - Join

Chapter 6

- Ordering
    - OrderBy
    - OrderByDescending
    - ThenBy
    - ThenByDescending
    - Reverse
- Partitioning
    - Skip
    - SkipWhile
    - Take
    - TakeWhile
- Projection
    - Select
    - SelectMany
- Quantifiers
    - All
    - Any
    - Contains
- Restriction
    - Where
- Set
    - Distinct
    - Except
    - Intersect
    - Union

> Most standard query operators operate on a sequence where the later is an object of type `IEnumerable<T>` or the `IQueryable<T>` interfaces. The standard query operators can be divided into two groups. One group works on objects of type `IEnumerable<T>` and the other group works with objects of type `IQueryable<T>`.

Aggregation

You can use the aggregation operator Sum in a LINQ to Entities query as shown here:

```
using (PayrollEntities entities = new PayrollEntities())
    {
        var query = from s in entities.Salary
                    where entities.Salary.Sum(sal => s.Basic + s.Allowances) >= 15000
                    select s;
        foreach (Salary salary in query)
        {
            Response.Write("<BR>" + salary.Employee.EmployeeName);
        }
    }
```

The above query returns the names of employees whose total salary exceeds 15000.

Similarly, you can use the Count operator to display the total number of records retrieved from the above query as shown in the code snippet below:

```
using (PayrollEntities entities = new PayrollEntities())
    {
        var query = (from s in entities.Salary
                    where entities.Salary.Sum(sal => s.Basic + s.Allowances) >= 15000
                    select s).Count();
        Response.Write("Total no of records: " + query.ToString());
    }
```

Projections

The query below illustrates how you can create a projection of a new entity that contains the gross salary of employees, which includes the total of the allowances and basic:

```
using (PayrollEntities entities = new PayrollEntities())
    {
        var query = from s in entities.Salary
                    where entities.Salary.Sum(sal => s.Basic + s.Allowances) >= 150000
                    select new {Gross = s.Allowances + s.Basic};
        foreach (var v in query)
            Response.Write("<BR>" + v.Gross);
    }
```

Ordering

You can also order the result set in ascending or descending order. Here is a code snippet that illustrates how you can do this:

```
using (PayrollEntities entities = new PayrollEntities())
    {
        var query = from s in entities.Salary
                    where entities.Salary.Sum(sal => s.Basic + s.Allowances) >= 150000
                    select new { Gross = s.Allowances + s.Basic };
        foreach (var v in query.OrderByDescending(x=>x.Gross))
            Response.Write("<BR>" + v.Gross);
    }
```

Here is how you can use the `orderby` operator in your LINQ to Entities query to order the resultset in ascending order of employee names:

```
using (PayrollEntities entities = new PayrollEntities())
    {
        ObjectQuery<Employee> employees = entities.Employee;
        IQueryable<Employee> sortedEmployees =
            from emp in employees
          orderby emp.EmployeeName
            select emp;
        foreach (Employee employeeMaster in sortedEmployees)
            Response.Write("<BR>" + employeeMaster.EmployeeName);
    }
```

Quantifiers

A quantifier operation returns a boolean value indicative of whether or not one or more elements in a sequence satisfies a particular condition. Here is the list of the quantifier operations that can be performed by the standard query operators:

- All
- Any
- Contains

You can use any of the quantifiers such as All, Any or Contains to search for a sequence. As an example, the following query returns true or false depending on whether all employees who reside in Hyderabad joined the organization in January:

```
var query = (from emp in entities.Employee
    where emp.EmployeeAddress == "Hyderabad"
    select emp).All(emp => emp.JoiningDate.Month == 1);
```

Similarly, you can change the above query to return either a true or a false value depending on whether any employee in the organization joined in January and resides in the UK:

```
var query = (from emp in entities.Employee
    where emp.EmployeeAddress == "UK"
    select emp).Any(emp => emp.JoiningDate.Month == 1);
```

Restriction

You can restrict the results of a LINQ to Entities query based on a certain condition. Doing this requires the `where` operator. Here is an example that illustrates how you can use the `where` operator to restrict the results in your resultset to the condition that you have specified in your query:

```
using (PayrollEntities entities = new PayrollEntities())
    {
        ObjectQuery<Employee> employees = entities.Employee;
        IQueryable<Employee> employee =
            from emp in employees
            where emp.EmployeeAddress == "UK"
            select emp;
        foreach (Employee employeeMaster in employees)
            Response.Write("<BR>" + employeeMaster.EmployeeName);
    }
```

When you execute the above query, only the names of employees residing in the UK are listed.

Conversion

You can use the conversion operators like `ToList` or `ToArray` on your LINQ to Entities query to convert the resultset to a collection of `List` or `Array` type. Here is an example that illustrates how you can use the `ToList` operator:

```
using (PayrollEntities payrollEntities = new PayrollEntities())
    {
        ObjectQuery<Salary> salary = payrollEntities.Salary;
        IList result = (from s in salary
            select s.Employee).ToList();
        foreach (Employee emp in result)
            Response.Write("<BR>"+emp.EmployeeName);
    }
```

Similarly, you can use the `ToArray` operator to covert the same resultset to a collection of type array as shown in the code snippet below:

```
using (PayrollEntities payrollEntities = new PayrollEntities())
    {
        ObjectQuery<Salary> salary = payrollEntities.Salary;
        Array result = (from s in salary
                        select s.Employee).ToArray();
        foreach (Employee emp in result)
            Response.Write("<BR>"+emp.EmployeeName);
    }
```

Element

You can use the `First` or the `Last` operator to retrieve the first or last object in a sequence as shown below:

```
using (PayrollEntities entities = new PayrollEntities())
    {
        var query = (from emp in entities.Employee
                     where emp.EmployeeAddress == "UK"
                     select emp).First();
        Response.Write(query.EmployeeName);
    }
```

Set

Here is an example that uses the `Distinct` operator to display the employee names stored in the Salary table:

```
using (PayrollEntities payrollEntities = new PayrollEntities())
    {
        ObjectQuery<Salary> salary = payrollEntities.Salary;
        IQueryable<Employee> result = (from s in salary
        select s.Employee).Distinct();
        foreach (Employee emp in result)
            Response.Write("<BR>"+emp.EmployeeName);
    }
```

Working with LINQ to Entities

Querying Data Using LINQ

Let us take a look at how we can use LINQ to query data in our applications. The following code snippet illustrates how you can use LINQ to display the contents of an array:

```
String[] employees = {"Joydip", "Douglas", "Jini", "Piku", "Amal",
                      "Rama", "Indronil"};
var employeeNames = from employee in employees select employee;
foreach (var empName in employeeNames)
    Response.Write(empName);
```

Let us now discuss how to use LINQ to query a generic list. Consider the Generic Employee List given below:

```
private static List<String> GenericEmployeeList = new List<String>()
{
  "Joydip", "Douglas", "Jini", "Piku",
  "Rama", "Amal", "Indronil"
};
```

You can use LINQ to query this list as shown in the following code snippet:

```
IEnumerable<String> employees = from emp in GenericEmployeeList
   select emp;
foreach (string employee in employees)
{
  Response.Write(employee);
}
```

You can use conditions with your LINQ query as well. The following example shows how:

```
IEnumerable<String> employees = from emp in GenericEmployeeList where
emp.Length > 4 select emp;
  foreach (string employee in employees)
  {
    Response.Write(employee);
  }
```

In this code snippet, we use LINQ to display the employee names more than 4 characters in length. The above query displays the following output:

```
Joydip
Douglas
Indronil
```

Here is another example of how you can use conditional queries with LINQ. To display the names of employees whose names start with the letter "J", you can use the following:

```
IEnumerable<String> employees = from emp in GenericEmployeeList where
    emp.StartsWith("J")
    select emp;
foreach (String employee in employees)
{
  Response.Write(employee);
}
```

This code snippet will result in the following employee names being displayed:

```
Joydip
Jini
```

As you can see from the above output, only those employees whose names start with the letter "J" are displayed.

The following code snippet illustrates how you can use LINQ to Datasets to retrieve the details of specific employees from a `DataTable` instance which contains a collection of employees:

```
DataTable empDataTable = new DataTable();
empDataTable.Columns.Add("EmpCode", typeof(String));
empDataTable.Columns.Add("EmpName", typeof(String));
empDataTable.Columns.Add("DeptCode", typeof(String));
empDataTable.Columns.Add("Salary", typeof(Decimal));
empDataTable.Rows.Add("E0001", "Joydip", "D0001",23000);
empDataTable.Rows.Add("E0002", "Douglas", "D0002", 45000);
empDataTable.Rows.Add("E0003", "Jini", "D0001", 12000);
empDataTable.Rows.Add("E0004", "Piku", "D0003", 13000);
empDataTable.Rows.Add("E0005", "Rama", "D0003", 27500);
empDataTable.Rows.Add("E0006", "Amal", "D0002", 19500);

var empRecords = from row in empDataTable.AsEnumerable()
   where row.Field<decimal>("Salary") > 15000
       select row;

foreach (var emp in empRecords)
Response.Write("<BR>"+emp["EmpCode"].ToString() + "\t" +
emp["EmpName"].ToString() + "\t" + emp["Salary"].ToString());
```

Working with LINQ to Entities

We will now demonstrate how to use LINQ to query data from a generic list. Here is the code that illustrates how to do this:

```
List<Employee> empList = new List<Employee>()
{
        new Employee
        {
            EmpCode = "E0001", EmpName = "Joydip", DeptCode =
                    "D0001", Salary = 23000
        },
        new Employee
        {
            EmpCode = "E0002", EmpName = "Douglas", DeptCode =
                    "D0003", Salary = 45000
        },
        new Employee
        {
            EmpCode = "E0003", EmpName = "Jini", DeptCode = "D0002",
                    Salary = 15000
        }
};
var empRecords = from row in empList.AsEnumerable()
   where row.Salary > 15000
        select row;
foreach (var emp in empRecords)
    Response.Write("<BR>" + emp.EmpCode.ToString() + "\t" +
      emp.EmpName.ToString() + "\t" + emp.Salary.ToString());
```

Here is the code for our Employee class:

```
public class Employee
{
    public string EmpCode { get; set;}
    public string EmpName { get; set;}
    public string DeptCode { get; set;}
    public DateTime JoiningDate { get; set;}
    public decimal Salary { get; set;}
}
```

Required Namespaces

You should include the System.Linq namespace if you want to use LINQ for SQL, LINQ to XML, or LINQ to Objects. For using Lamda expressions, you should include the System.Linq.Expressions namespace.

Expressions in LINQ to Entities

An expression in LINQ is a piece of code that can be evaluated to one of the following:

- Single value
- Object
- Method

Expressions will contain one of the following:

- A literal
- An operator
- A method call

The results of LINQ to Entities queries are returned as one of the following:

- Entity Data Model compatible CLR types
- Collection of one or more entity instances
- `IQueryable` instances
- `IGrouping` instances
- Anonymous types

 To use expressions in LINQ to entities, you need to include the System.Linq.Expressions namespace in your programs.

Here is an example that illustrates how an expression can be used:

```
IQueryable<string> employeeContact = from emp in employee
where emp.City = "Hyderabad" select emp.EmpName;
```

In the above example, employee is an instance of the Employee class. It is a business object that relates to the entity called Employee. The above query will return the names of all employees who live in Hyderabad.

Constant Expressions

Constant expressions are used to evaluate constant values. These expressions are evaluated to constant command tree expressions directly. Here is an example that illustrates how constant expressions are evaluated:

```
using (PayrollEntities payrollContext = new PayrollEntities())
        {
                ObjectQuery<Salary> salary = payrollEntities.Salary;
                IQueryable<string> salaryInfo =
                    from s in SalaryMaster
                    where s.Basic >= 5000 + 1000
                    select s.EmployeeID;
                foreach (String empID in salaryInfo)
                {
                    Console.WriteLine(empID);
                }
        }
```

The above query lists the EmployeeIDs of employees having Basic greater than or equal to 6000. Note that the value 1000 in the above query represents a constant.

Comparison Expressions

A comparison expression is used to check whether a constant, a property, or a result from a method call is equal to, not equal to, greater than, or less than another value. Refer to the code snippet below that illustrates how such expressions can be used:

```
using (PayrollEntities payrollContext = new PayrollEntities())
        {
                ObjectQuery<Salary> salary = payrollEntities.Salary;
                IQueryable<string> salaryInfo =
                    from s in SalaryMaster
                    where s.Basic <= 15000
                    select s.EmployeeID;
                foreach (String empID in salaryInfo)
                {
                    Console.WriteLine(empID);
                }
        }
```

The above query will list the EmployeeIDs of employees whose Basic is less than or equal to 15000.

The code snippet given below illustrates how you can use comparison expressions to display the names of the employees who work in the HR department:

```
PayrollEntities payrollEntities = new PayrollModel.PayrollEntities();
    var result = from emp in payrollEntities.Employee where emp.DepartmentMaster.DepartmentName == "HR" select emp;
    foreach (Employee e in result)
    {
        Response.Write("<BR>" + e.EmployeeName);
    }
```

The following example shows how you can display the names of all employees who have joined the organization on or after a specified date:

```
using (PayrollEntities payrollContext = new PayrollEntities())
        {
            DateTime joiningDate =
              new DateTime(2004, 1, 1);
            ObjectQuery<Employee> employee =
            payrollEntities.Employee;
            IQueryable<string> employeeInfo =
                from emp in Employee
                where emp.JoiningDate >= joiningDate
                select emp.EmpName;
            foreach (String empName in employeeInfo)
            {
                Console.WriteLine(empID);
            }
        }
```

The above query will list the names of all employees who have joined the organization on or after January 1, 2004.

Initializing Expressions

Initialization Expressions are used to initialize a new instance. The following code snippet illustrates how you can use Initialization Expressions to compose and initialize a new instance:

```
using (PayrollEntities payrollContext = new PayrollEntities())
        {
            DateTime joiningDate =
              new DateTime(2004, 1, 1);
            ObjectQuery<Employee> employee =
```

```
                payrollEntities.Employee;
        IQueryable<string> employeeInfo =
            from emp in Employee
            where emp.JoiningDate >= joiningDate
            select new {emp.EmpName, emp.JoiningDate};
        foreach (var e in employeeInfo)
        {
            Console.WriteLine("Name: "+e.EmpName+"\t"+"Joining
  Date: "+e.JoiningDate);
        }
    }
```

When you execute the above query, the names and joining dates of the employees who have joined the organization on or after January 1, 2004 will be listed.

> A query in LINQ is a generic query. Namely, it is of type ObjectQuery<T>, a class that implements the IQueryable and IEnumerable<T> interfaces. When the query is executed, that is, when you enumerate or iterate through the collection a generic ObjectResult an object of type ObjectResult<T> is returned. Actually, ObjectQuery represents the query prior to its execution. ObjectResult on the other hand, represents the same after the query has been executed.

Null Comparisons

Consider a column called **Tax** in the **Employee** table. The value for this column will be null for employees having no tax, or will display the taxable amount to be deducted otherwise. Here is a **T-SQL** statement that illustrates how you perform null comparisons:

```
SELECT EmpName from Employee where Tax is null
```

The above query lists the names of all employees who don't fall into the tax bracket. In other words, their salary is not taxable.

The same can be done in LINQ as shown here:

```
var result = from emp in payrollEntities.Employee where emp.Tax ==
null select emp.EmpName;
```

Navigation Properties

Navigation properties enable you to navigate from one end of an entity to another. In essence, you can use them to locate entities at the end of an association.

Consider the custom entity class called `EmployeeContact` given below:

```
public class EmployeeContact
{
    private String name;
    private String address;
    public string Name
    {
        get
        {
            return name;
        }
        set
        {
            name = value;
        }
    }
    public string Address
    {
        get
        {
            return address;
        }
        set
        {
            address = value;
        }
    }
}
```

We will now see how to use navigation properties to compose a collection of instances of this class using LINQ to Entities. Here is the code:

```
PayrollEntities payrollEntities = new PayrollModel.PayrollEntities();
        IQueryable<EmployeeContact> query = payrollEntities.Employee
        .Where(emp => emp.JoiningDate >= new DateTime(2004,01,01))
        .Select(emp => new EmployeeContact { Name = emp.EmployeeName,
    Address = emp.EmployeeAddress });
```

Working with LINQ to Entities

What did we do? We created an instance of our ObjectContext called
`PayrollEntities` and then we used a query to retrieve the names and addresses of
those employees who have joined the organization on or after January 1, 2004. We
composed instances of the `EmployeeContact` entity with the results retrieved.

 We can also use the Load () method to load related entities.

Now that our `IQueryable` instance contains a collection of `EmployeeContact`
instances, we can iterate through the collection of `EmployeeContact` instances and
display the values as shown:

```
foreach (EmployeeContact empContact in query)
{
    Response.Write("<BR>" + empContact.Name+" "+empContact.Address);
}
```

Immediate and Deferred Query Execution

Once a LINQ query is created and executed, it is converted into a command tree.
This is a representation of the query that is compatible with the ADO.NET Entity
Framework. Note that the LINQ to Entities queries are executed at the time the
results are iterated. Such an execution is also referred to as **Deferred Execution**. The
query is executed each time you iterate over the query variable inside of a loop. On
the contrary, **Immediate Execution** occurs when the queries return a single value
computed, or otherwise. Examples of such queries are when `Min`, `Max`, `Count`, and
`Average` are used to compute results. You can also force immediate execution of a
query by invoking the `ToList()` or `ToArray()` methods on a query or query instance.

Here are two methods. The first illustrates immediate execution and the second one
illustrates deferred execution:

```
public static void ImmediateExecution()
    {
        int[] intArray = new int[] { 1, 2, 3, 4, 5};
        int index = 0;
        var query = from i in intArray select ++index;
        Console.WriteLine("Illustrating Immediate Execution\n");
        foreach (var number in query)
            Console.WriteLine("The value of number is: {0}. The value of index is: {1}", number, index);
    }
public static void DeferredExecution()
```

[148]

```
        {
            int[] intArray = new int[] { 1, 2, 3, 4, 5 };
            int index = 0;
            var query = (from i in intArray select ++index).ToList();
            Console.WriteLine("\n\nIllustrating Deferred Execution\n");
            foreach (var number in query)
                Console.WriteLine("The value of number is: {0}. The value of index is: {1}", number, index);
        }
```

The following code will invoke both these methods one by one as shown in the code snippet below:

```
ImmediateExecution();
DeferredExecution();
Console.WriteLine("\nPress any key...");
Console.Read();
```

When you execute the program, the output looks like the following figure:

```
Illustrating Immediate Execution

The value of number is: 1. The value of index is: 1
The value of number is: 2. The value of index is: 2
The value of number is: 3. The value of index is: 3
The value of number is: 4. The value of index is: 4
The value of number is: 5. The value of index is: 5

Illustrating Deferred Execution

The value of number is: 1. The value of index is: 5
The value of number is: 2. The value of index is: 5
The value of number is: 3. The value of index is: 5
The value of number is: 4. The value of index is: 5
The value of number is: 5. The value of index is: 5

Press any key...
```

As you can see from the above figure, the value of the variable index increments with each iteration in the first method call but does not change in the second method call. Why? In the second method, we have made a call to the method `ToList()` that generates a list with the query results. This is an example of deferred query execution in contrast to the first method. As a result, the list is prepared with the maximum value of the variable called **index**. In our example, the maximum possible value of index is 5.

Improving Performance with Compiled Queries

LINQ to Entities queries are re-compiled before they are executed each time. This becomes a performance constraint that can be overcome using Compiled Queries. Note that Compiled Queries are compiled only once. This happens the first time they are called. For each subsequent call, the query plan is retrieved from the Query Plan Cache. This improves performance in subsequent calls. Here is an example that illustrates how compiled queries can be used:

```
var employees = CompiledQuery.Compile((PayrollEntities entities,
string address) =>
        from employee in entities.Employee
        where employee.EmployeeAddress.Equals(address)
            orderby employee.EmployeeName
                select employee);
    using (PayrollEntities payrollEntities = new
PayrollEntities())
    {
        foreach (var employee in employees(payrollEntities,
"Kolkata"))
        {
            Response.Write("<BR>"+employee.EmployeeName);
        }
    }
```

The example above displays the names of all employees who reside in Kolkata. Note that you should have at least one parameter in a compiled query. This is the ObjectContext.

Summary

In this chapter, we discussed LINQ to Entities and how it can be used to query data against the Entity Data Model. We looked at the standard query operators and expressions in LINQ and how they can be used. We have also discussed two of the most important features in LINQ, namely, immediate and deferred query execution and compiled queries. In the next chapter, we will explore the ObjectServices layer of the Entity Framework and discuss how it can be used in our applications. We will also see how we can use LINQ with Object Services to query data in our applications. So, stay tuned!

7
Working with the Object Services Layer

In this chapter, we will discuss Object Services and it can be used to perform **CRUD** operations against the **Entity Data Model**. **Object Services** provide services such as identity resolution, change tracking, object persistency, and also update processing. The **Object Services Layer** internally uses an **Object Query** object for query processing. To use Object Services, you should include the `System.Data.Objects` and `System.Data.Objects.DataClasses` namespaces.

In this chapter, we will discuss the following:

- An introduction to Object Services
- Using Object Services to perform CRUD operations
- Handling data concurrency conflicts using `ObjectContext`
- Inheritance in the Entity Data Model

What are Object Services?

Object Services enable you to work with entities such as memory objects. It strives to eliminate the impedance mismatch that exists between the relational or logical and the programming models. You can use Object Services for change tracking, data binding objects to data controls, and handling concurrency conflicts. Object Services support both LINQ and Entity SQL queries. The classes of the Object Services Layer is contained is the System.Data.Objects and System.Data.Objects.DataClasses namespaces. The ObjectContext is the core of the Object Services Layer.

Working with the Object Services Layer

The `ObjectContext` class encapsulates the following:

- An `EntityConnection` instance
- A `MetadataWorkspace` instance
- An instance of `ObjectStateManager`

While the `EntityConnection` instance is responsible for connecting to the database, the instance of `MetadataWorkspace` contains the metadata information that describes the entity data model. The `ObjectContext` class also encapsulates an `ObjectStateManager` instance that enables you to track an object's state while a CRUD operation is performed.

The `ObjectContext` is the gateway to the EMD. You use it to connect to the model and perform CRUD operations. You can use it to read data using the `CreateQuery()` method, add entities using the `AddObject()` method, delete entities using the `DeleteObject()` method, persist the changes to the database using the `Save()` method and attach or detach entities to and from the `ObjectContext` using the `Attach()` and `Detach()` methods respectively.

You should use the `EntityClient` when you would like to use dynamic queries or use the ADO.NET style of interacting with your databases for performing CRUD operations. Use LINQ to Entities when you would like to use strongly typed queries. You should use Object Services when you would like to explore the powerful features of the Object Services Layer. This might include tracking and identity resolution, efficient ways to managing transactions, object serialization, and queries that are not checked at compile time.

Why do we require a specific `ObjectContext` class like `PayrollEntities`, when we already have an `ObjectContext` class? The `ObjectContext` class provided by the Entity Framework library provides the basic features stated above. If you are to provide some specific behavior, like add employee objects or query employee objects from the EDM, you have to inherit your specific `ObjectContext` class, like PayrollEntities, from the base `ObjectContext` class to incorporate this behavior. This would enable you to query the EDM using statements such as:

    payrollContext.CreateQuery<Employee>("[Employee]")

Or add new entities to the `ObjectContext` using statements such as:

    payrollContext.AddObject("Employee",employeeObject)

Features at a Glance

Here are some of the striking features of Object Services at a glance:

- Querying data as objects
- Support for Change Tracking and Identity Resolution
- Data merging
- Object serialization
- Transaction management
- Support for entity persistence
- Querying data with LINQ or Entity SQL
- Support for Entity Inheritance
- Support for Deferred Execution

A Quick Look at the ObjectContext Class in our Payroll EDM

In this section, we will take a look at how the `ObjectContext` class is organized. Here is how the `ObjectContext` class for our Payroll EDM looks:

```
    public partial class PayrollEntities : global::System.Data.
Objects.ObjectContext
    {
        public PayrollEntities() :
                base("name=PayrollEntities", "PayrollEntities")
        {
        }
        public PayrollEntities(string connectionString) :
                base(connectionString, "PayrollEntities")
        {
        }
        public PayrollEntities(global::System.Data.EntityClient.
EntityConnection connection) :
                base(connection, "PayrollEntities")
        {
        }
        [global::System.ComponentModel.BrowsableAttribute(false)]
        public global::System.Data.Objects.ObjectQuery<Department> 
Department
        {
            get
            {
```

Working with the Object Services Layer

```
                if ((this._Department == null))
                {
                    this._Department = base.CreateQuery<Department>
("[Department]");
                }
                return this._Department;
            }
        }
        private global::System.Data.Objects.ObjectQuery<Department>
_Department;
        [global::System.ComponentModel.BrowsableAttribute(false)]
        public global::System.Data.Objects.ObjectQuery<Designation>
Designation
        {
            get
            {
                if ((this._Designation == null))
                {
                    this._Designation = base.CreateQuery<Designation>
("[Designation]");
                }
                return this._Designation;
            }
        }
        private global::System.Data.Objects.ObjectQuery<Designation>
_Designation;
        [global::System.ComponentModel.BrowsableAttribute(false)]
        public global::System.Data.Objects.ObjectQuery<Employee>
Employee
        {
            get
            {
                if ((this._Employee == null))
                {
                    this._Employee = base.CreateQuery<Employee>
("[Employee]");
                }
                return this._Employee;
            }
        }
        private global::System.Data.Objects.ObjectQuery<Employee>
_Employee;
        [global::System.ComponentModel.BrowsableAttribute(false)]
        public global::System.Data.Objects.ObjectQuery<ProvidentFund>
ProvidentFund
        {
            get
```

```csharp
            {
                if ((this._ProvidentFund == null))
                {
                    this._ProvidentFund = base.CreateQuery<ProvidentFund>("[ProvidentFund]");
                }
                return this._ProvidentFund;
            }
        }
        private global::System.Data.Objects.ObjectQuery<ProvidentFund> _ProvidentFund;
        [global::System.ComponentModel.BrowsableAttribute(false)]
        public global::System.Data.Objects.ObjectQuery<Salary> Salary
        {
            get
            {
                if ((this._Salary == null))
                {
                    this._Salary = base.CreateQuery<Salary>("[Salary]");
                }
                return this._Salary;
            }
        }
        private global::System.Data.Objects.ObjectQuery<Salary> _Salary;
        public void AddToEmployee(Employee employee)
        {
            base.AddObject("Employee", employee);
        }
        public void AddToDepartment(Department department)
        {
            base.AddObject("Department", department);
        }
        public void AddToSalary(Salary salary)
        {
            base.AddObject("Salary", salary);
        }
        public void AddToDesignation(Designation designation)
        {
            base.AddObject("Designation", designation);
        }
        public void AddToProvidentFund(ProvidentFund providentFund)
        {
            base.AddObject("ProvidentFund", providentFund);
        }
    }
```

As you can see from the above code, `PayrollEntities` is our `ObjectContext` class that derives from `ObjectContext` class of the `System.Data.Objects` namespace. You can see a list of overloaded constructors that call the constructor of the base class and pass the container name and connection string as parameters. This is followed by a list of properties of type `ObjectQuery` that correspond to each of the entities we have in our Payroll EDM. Next, we have a list of Add methods: `AddToEmployee()`, `AddToDepartment()`, `AddToSalary()`, `AddToProvidentFund()`, and `AddToDesignation()` which add these entities in the `ObjectContext`. These methods call the `AddObject()` method of the base class, internally, and pass the entity set name and entity instances as parameters.

Querying Data as in-Memory Objects

Object Services are used to work with your entities as in-memory objects, or a collection of in-memory objects. The Object Services Layer internally uses an `ObjectQuery` object for query processing and supports querying data using both Entity SQL and LINQ. The `ObjectQuery` class implements the `IQueryable<T>` and `IEnumerable<T>` generic interfaces.

Queries are created using the `ObjectQuery` class that internally contains a list of query builder methods. Upon execution, the `ObjectQuery` instance returns the result set in terms of an instance of `ObjectResult`. Note that the query you executed using `ObjectQuery` is executed late. That is, it is executed only after you enumerate the `ObjectResult` instance. This deferred execution is a great feature of the Object Services Layer.

The basic reason for using Object Services is that you can program against objects, such as storing and retrieving objects or collections of objects, to and from any data store while writing much less code.

Adding, Modifying, and Deleting Objects

In this section, we will discuss how you can use `ObjectServices` to add, modify, and delete an object within an `ObjectContext`.

To add an object to the `ObjectContext` requires the use of the `AddObject` method. It accepts the entity set name and entity instance as parameters and adds the object passed to it to the `ObjectContext`. Once you have added an object to the `ObjectContext`, you can call the `SaveChanges` to persist the changes to the database.

Chapter 7

Here is an example that shows how you can add an object to the `ObjectContext` and then call the `SaveChanges` method to persist the changes to the database:

```
PayrollModel.PayrollEntities ctx = new PayrollModel.PayrollEntities();
PayrollModel.Employee employee = new PayrollModel.Employee();
employee.EmployeeID = 16;
employee.EmployeeName = "Debanjan Banerjee";
employee.EmployeeAddress = "Kolkata";
employee.JoiningDate = DateTime.Now;
employee.Department = ctx.Department.
Where(d => d.DepartmentID == 3).First();
ctx.AddObject("Employee", employee);
ctx.SaveChanges();
```

Here is an example that shows how you can use `ObjectContext` and **LINQ** to update a record in the database:

```
using (ObjectContext ctx = new ObjectContext("Name=PayrollEntities"))
      {
          var query = (from employee in ctx.
CreateQuery<PayrollModel.Employee>("PayrollEntities.Employee")
          select employee).Where(e=>e.EmployeeID == 16);
          foreach (PayrollModel.Employee emp in query)
          {
              emp.EmployeeAddress = "Chennai";
          }
          ctx.SaveChanges();
      }
```

To delete the record you just inserted, use the `DeleteObject()` method of the `ObjectContext` as shown in the code snippet below:

```
PayrollModel.PayrollEntities ctx = new PayrollModel.PayrollEntities();
PayrollModel.Employee employee =
ctx.Employee.Where(e => e.EmployeeID == 16).First();
ctx.DeleteObject(employee);
ctx.SaveChanges();
```

You can also modify an existing record. To do this, you first need to search the record to be deleted and then delete the object from the `ObjectContext`. Once deleted, you can now add a new object to the `ObjectContext` and call the `SaveChanges` method to update the changes in the database. Here is the code:

```
PayrollModel.PayrollEntities ctx = new PayrollModel.PayrollEntities();
PayrollModel.Employee employee =
ctx.Employee.Where(e => e.EmployeeID == 16).First();
ctx.DeleteObject(employee);
PayrollModel.Employee newRecord = new PayrollModel.Employee();
```

```
newRecord.EmployeeID = 16;
newRecord.EmployeeName = "Debanjan Banerjee";
newRecord.EmployeeAddress = "New Delhi";
newRecord.JoiningDate = DateTime.Now;
newRecord.Department = ctx.Department.
Where(d => d.DepartmentID == 4).First();
ctx.AddObject("Employee", newRecord);
ctx.SaveChanges();
```

Attaching and Detaching Objects to and from the Object Context

You can use the `Attach` or `Detach` methods of the `ObjectContext` to attach or detach objects. It should be noted that `Attach` will attach the entire object graph. The method cannot determine which objects are new and which already exist in the `ObjectContext`. Note that when you execute a query on the `ObjectContext`, the objects that are returned as a result of the query are attached in the `ObjectContext`. You can attach an object to the `ObjectContext` by calling any of the following methods on the `ObjectContext`:

- Attach
- AddObject
- AttachTo
- ApplyPropertyChanges

But what does `Attach` and `Detach` mean here? You use `Attach` to attach an object to the context. You should use `Attach` when the entity already exists in the database want the context to know about it without doing a query to locate the entity. When you attach an entity to the `ObjectContext` using the `Attach` method, it sets the `EntityState` of the object being attached to `Unchanged`. In other words, these objects switch to an un-modified state in the `ObjectContext`.

On the contrary, if the entity in question is new and is not present in the context, and you also want to insert data into your database, then you should use Add. Here is how you can use the `Attach` method on the `ObjectContext` to attach an object:

```
ctx.Attach(department);
```

Now, the `Employee` object and `Department` object have a relationship between them. If you were to attach the `Department` object to the `Employee` object, you would use the following code:

```
payrollContext.Attach(detachedEmployee);
detachedEmployee.Department.Add(department);
```

You can also use the `ObjectContext` to attach objects, even objects that were detached from the `ObjectContext` earlier. When you no longer need an object to be referenced in your `ObjectContext`, you can detach it. Note that detached objects are de-referenced. In other words, they are not referenced by the `ObjectContext` any more. So, you can detach objects when they are no longer needed to facilitate garbage collection. You can detach objects from the `ObjectContext` by calling the `Detach` method as shown below:

```
ctx.Detach(ctx.Department.First());
```

You can also attach a detached instance. Here is how you can attach a detached employee object.

```
payrollContext.Attach(detachedEmployee);
```

The `AttachTo()` method is used to attach an object, or an object graph into the object context in an un-changed state. You can use this method to attach entity objects, or graphs of entity objects, if the object being added is null, a single object, or an object that is a part of the object graph. Here is how this method can be used in code:

```
payrollContext.AttachTo("Employee",employeeObject);
```

 When you execute a query inside an object context, the objects that are returned by the query are all attached to the object context in use.

Serializing and De-Serializing Entity Instances

You can serialize or de-serialize an entity instance using the `ObjectContext`. To do this, you need to call the `Serialize` or the `Deserialize` method of the `BinaryFormatter` class as shown in the code snippets below:

```
private void Serialize(String fileName,Object obj)
    {
        BinaryFormatter binaryFormatter = new BinaryFormatter();
        FileStream fileStream = new FileStream(fileName,FileMode.Create);
            try
            {
                binaryFormatter.Serialize(fileStream, obj);
            }
            catch (SerializationException ex)
            {
```

```
                    throw new ApplicationException("The object graph could
    not be serialized", ex);
            }
            finally
            {
                fileStream.Close();
            }
        }
```

The `Serialize` method shown above accepts a file name and the object to be serialized as parameters, serializes it using a `BinaryFormatter` instance, and then stores the serialized instance of the file.

Here is the `DeSerialize` method that accepts the name of the file where the serialized instance is stored and returns the de-serialized instance back:

```
        public Object DeSerialize(String fileName)
        {
            BinaryFormatter binaryFormatter = new BinaryFormatter();
            FileStream fileStream = new FileStream(fileName, FileMode.Open);
            try
            {
                fileStream.Seek(0, SeekOrigin.Begin);
                return binaryFormatter.Deserialize(fileStream);
            }
            catch (SerializationException ex)
            {
                throw new ApplicationException("Serialization Exception: " + ex.Message);
            }
            finally
            {
                fileStream.Close();
            }
            return null;
        }
```

The following code shows how you can use the `Serialize` and `De-Serialize` methods we defined earlier:

```
Employee employee;
using (PayrollModel.PayrollEntities ctx = new PayrollModel.PayrollEntities())
{
ObjectQuery<PayrollModel.Employee> query = null;
query = ctx.CreateQuery<PayrollModel.Employee>(@"SELECT VALUE e FROM PayrollEntities.Employee AS e");
```

```
employee = query.Where(emp => emp.EmployeeID == 1).First();
Serialize("C:\\Test\\Test.txt",employee);
}
```

The above code serializes the instance of the first employee of the Employee table and stores the serialized instance in the `Test.txt` file. Now, to de-serialize the instance and get back the original instance, you need to call the `DeSerialize` method as shown below:

```
Employee employee = (Employee)DeSerialize("C:\\Test\\Test.txt");
Response.Write("Employee Name: " + employee.EmployeeName);
Response.Write("<BR>Employee Address: " + employee.EmployeeAddress);
```

The following screenshot shows the employee name and address of the de-serialized employee instance:

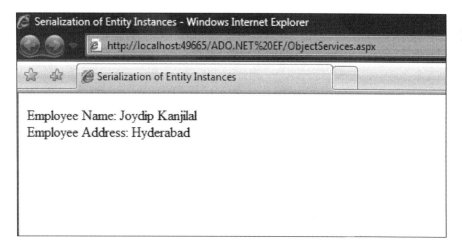

Change Tracking and Identity Resolution Using ObjectContext

Change Tracking in the Entity Framework is a feature that enables you detect and resolve conflicts that arise out of concurrent data updates on a particular entity. Such scenarios are commonly known as concurrency conflicts.

Two ways to handle data concurrencies in a multi-user environment are:

- Optimistic
- Pessimistic

In the Optimistic mode, the record is read but not locked. You need to check whether a record to be saved has already been modified. In essence, you need to track the changes in the data before you do any changes.

In the Pessimistic mode, the record being modified is locked from other users until the lock on the record is released. Therefore, Pessimistic concurrency is not a good choice, especially when you have a large number of users accessing the application at the same point in time.

By default, the Entity Framework follows the Optimistic concurrency model. When the **Object Services** layer saves the changes in an object to the database due to a call to its SaveChanges method, any checks for concurrency is bypassed. In other words, it does not check if there are any concurrency conflicts in the database.

You can, however, set the ConcurrencyMode attribute of an entity property in the conceptual layer to enable the Object Services layer to check for concurrency violations when it tries to save changes to the data back to the database. Here is how you can set the ConcurrencyMode attribute of an entity property:

```
<Property Name="EmployeeName" Type="String" Nullable="false"
MaxLength="50" Unicode="false"  ConcurrencyMode="Fixed"/>
```

If the ConcurrencyMode attribute is set for an entity in the EDM, the Object Services layer will always check for changes in the database before it saves the data in the database. When any conflict occurs, an OptimisticConcurrencyException will be thrown.

Implementing a Sample Application

In this section, we will implement a simple application that will demonstrate how we can use the ConcurrencyMode attribute in the **Entity Data Model** to detect any concurrency violation in the Employee table and display a message if a violation occurs.

Creating the Form

Before we begin discussing how data concurrency will work, let's get our form up and running.

Chapter 7

1. Add the following controls to your form:

Control	Name	Text
Label	lblMessage	
Label	lblEmpName	Employee Name
Label	lblEmpAddress	Employee Address
TextBox	txtName	
TextBox	txtAddress	
TextBox	txtJoiningDate	
DropDownList	ddlEmployee	Select Employee
Button	btnSave	Save Record
Button	btnRefresh	Refresh

When you view the web page in its design view, it will look like the figure below:

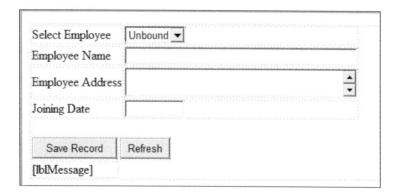

You are restricted to updating the employee name and address only. In other words, you can't update the joining date of the employee in this application. How is this done? Simple, we set the Enabled property of the `txtJoiningDate` TextBox control to false in the mark-up code.

Working with the Object Services Layer

2. Attach an event handler called `drpDept_SelectedIndexChanged` to the `drpDept DropDownList` control in its `onselectedindexchanged` event:

   ```
   <asp:DropDownList ID="ddlEmployee" runat="server"  AutoPostBack =
                                                      "true"
   onselectedindexchanged="ddlEmployee_SelectedIndexChanged">
   </asp:DropDownList>

   protected void ddlEmployee_SelectedIndexChanged(object sender,
                                                   EventArgs e)
       {

       }
   ```

3. Attach another event handler called `btnSave_Click` to the btnSave button control in its onclick event:

   ```
   protected void btnSave_Click(object sender, EventArgs e)
       {

       }
   ```

4. Now, enter the code for the `ddlEmployee_SelectedIndexChanged` event handler:

   ```
   protected void ddlEmployee_SelectedIndexChanged(object sender,
                                                   EventArgs e)
   {
       RefreshControls();
       GetSelectedEmployeeDetails();
   }
   ```

Implementing a Custom DataContext

We will now implement our custom data context that we will use going forward.

We have inherited from the `PayrollEntities` data context and added a custom method called `GetEmployeeRecords` to retrieve the details of all employees from the Employee table. Here is the code:

```
using System;
using System.Data;
using System.Linq;
using System.Web.UI.WebControls;
using System.Data.EntityClient;
using System.Data.Objects;
public class PayrollDataContext : PayrollModel.PayrollEntities
{
```

```
    String connectionString;
    public PayrollDataContext()
    {
        connectionString = base.Connection.ConnectionString;
    }
    public String ConnectionString
    {
        get
        {
            return connectionString;
        }
    }
    public ObjectResult<PayrollModel.Employee> GetEmployeeRecords()
    {
        ObjectContext ctx = new ObjectContext("Name=PayrollEntities");
        ObjectQuery<PayrollModel.Employee> query =
        ctx.CreateQuery<PayrollModel.Employee>(@"SELECT VALUE e FROM
PayrollEntities.Employee AS e");
        ObjectResult<PayrollModel.Employee> result = query.
Execute(MergeOption.NoTracking);
        return result;
    }
}
```

Now, enter the code for the `RefreshControls` and `GetSelectedEmployee` methods:

```
    private void RefreshControls()
    {
       txtEmpName.Text = String.Empty;
       txtEmpAddress.Text = String.Empty;
       txtJoiningDate.Text = String.Empty;
    }
  private void GetSelectedEmployeeDetails()
    {
        int employeeID = Int32.tryParse(ddlEmployee.SelectedValue.
Trim(), out employeeID);
        PayrollDataContext ctx = new PayrollDataContext();
        ObjectResult<PayrollModel.Employee> result =
        ctx.GetEmployeeRecords();
        foreach (PayrollModel.Employee emp in result)
        {
            if (emp.EmployeeID == employeeID)
            {
                txtEmpName.Text = emp.EmployeeName;
```

```
                    txtEmpAddress.Text = emp.EmployeeAddress;
                    txtJoiningDate.Text =
                    emp.JoiningDate.Day.ToString().Trim() + "-" +
                    emp.JoiningDate.Month.ToString().Trim() + "-"+
                    emp.JoiningDate.Year.ToString().Trim();
            }
        }
    }
```

Now, let's add the code for the `Page_Load` event handler:

```
protected void Page_Load(object sender, EventArgs e)
    {
        if (!IsPostBack)
        {
            PayrollDataContext ctx = new PayrollDataContext();
            ddlEmployee.DataSource = ctx.GetEmployeeRecords();
            ddlEmployee.DataTextField = "EmployeeName";
            ddlEmployee.DataValueField = "EmployeeID";
            ddlEmployee.DataBind();

            RefreshControls();
            GetSelectedEmployeeDetails();
        }
```

When you execute the application, the output will be similar to what is shown in the figure below:

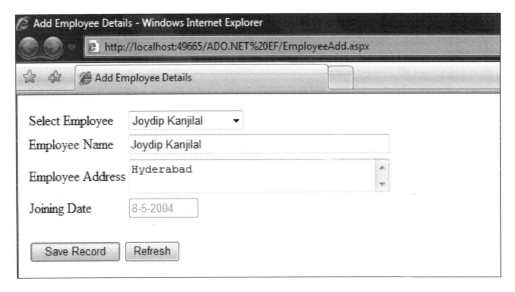

Now when you select a new employee from the employee DropDownList control, the details of the selected employee are displayed as seen in the following figure:

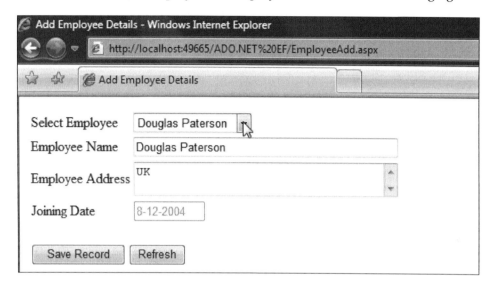

How is This Accomplished?

First, we added the controls to our form. We added a drop down list control to display the employee names, textboxes for the user to enter the employee details, buttons to save and refresh the entered data, and a label control to display messages based on the corresponding action that has occurred.

We added these methods into our code:

- `RefreshControls`
- `GetSelectedEmployeeDetails`

We also added two event handlers, the `ddlEmployee_SelectedIndexChanged` and `btnSave_Click`. We'll talk more about the `btnSave_Click` event handler later when we are ready to define it.

The `ddlEmployee_SelectedIndexChanged` event handler will be called when you select an employee from the `ddlEmployee` DropDownList control. This handler will do two things. First, it will refresh data of the controls in the form using the `RefreshControls()` method. Second, it will then make a call to the `GetSelectedEmployeeDetails` method.

Working with the Object Services Layer

The first thing that happens in the Page_Load event is that the employee DropDownList control is populated with the employee names:

```
PayrollDataContext ctx = new PayrollDataContext();
ddlEmployee.DataSource = ctx.GetEmployeeRecords();
ddlEmployee.DataTextField = "EmployeeName";
ddlEmployee.DataValueField = "EmployeeID";
ddlEmployee.DataBind();
```

Next, the `RefreshControls` and `GetSelectedEmployeeDetails` methods are called one after the other:

```
RefreshControls();
GetSelectedEmployeeDetails();
```

Note that the first time the web page is loaded, the details of the first employee selected will be displayed in the text box controls. By default, the selected index property of the employee drop down list control has a value of zero. You should set the Enabled property of the DropDownList control to false if there are no records in the database. You should then display an appropriate message to the user to avoid run time errors. Our example requires that there should be at least one record in the database table.

At this point, our form is functional in that it displays details of the selected employee. However, it obviously doesn't save anything yet!

Updating an Employee Record

We will now implement the code to update the selected employee details. To update an employee, you have to select the particular employee from the employee DropDownList control, edit the employee name or employee address, and then click on the Save button.

Here, we'll add the code for the `btnSave_Click` event handler:

```
protected void btnSave_Click(object sender, EventArgs e)
    {
        int employeeID = Int32.TryParse(ddlEmployee.SelectedValue.Trim(), out employeeID);
        PayrollModel.PayrollEntities ctx = new PayrollModel.PayrollEntities();
        try
        {
            PayrollModel.Employee employee =
                ctx.Employee.Where(emp => emp.EmployeeID == employeeID).First();
```

```
            employee.EmployeeName = txtEmpName.Text.Trim();
            employee.EmployeeAddress = txtEmpAddress.Text.Trim();
            ctx.SaveChanges();
            lblMessage.ForeColor = Color.Black;
            lblMessage.Text = "1 Record Saved";
        }
        catch (OptimisticConcurrencyException)
        {
            lblMessage.ForeColor = Color.Red;
            lblMessage.Text = "Concurrency violation occurred..";
        }
   }
```

The above code retrieves the Employee instance from the ObjectContext using the employee id of the employee selected. Next, the employee name and address are assigned to the Employee instance and the SaveChanges method is called.

When you execute this code, the employee record is successfully updated as shown in the following figure:

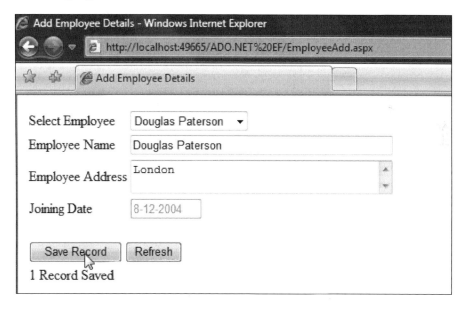

Working with the Object Services Layer

Handling Concurrency Conflicts

To handle concurrency conflicts you need to use the `ConcurrencyMode` property of the `EntityType`. Here are the steps to do this:

1. Open the `PayrollDataModel` in XML view and specify the `ConcurrencyMode` for the `EmployeeName` and `EmployeeAddress` properties of the Employee entity as `Fixed`. Here is the code:

   ```
   <EntityType Name="Employee">
         <Key>
           <PropertyRef Name="EmployeeID" />
         </Key>
         <Property Name="EmployeeID" Type="Int32" Nullable="false" />
         <Property Name="EmployeeName" Type="String" Nullable="false" MaxLength="50" Unicode="false" ConcurrencyMode="Fixed"/>
         <Property Name="EmployeeAddress" Type="String" Nullable="false" MaxLength="100" Unicode="false" ConcurrencyMode="Fixed"/>
         <Property Name="JoiningDate" Type="DateTime" Nullable="false" />
         <NavigationProperty Name="Department" Relationship="PayrollModel.FK_Employee_Department" FromRole="Employee" ToRole="Department" />
         <NavigationProperty Name="Salary" Relationship="PayrollModel.FK_Salary_Employee" FromRole="Employee" ToRole="Salary" />
      </EntityType>
   ```

> You can also change state of the object and then save it to create the concurrency conflict programmatically.

   When the application is executed again, no concurrency conflicts are detected as the employee record is saved. Now, let's do a trick now.

2. Set a break point to the statement, `ctx.SaveChanges();` in `btnSave_Click` event handler, and execute the program again by pressing F5. This time, as the break point has been set, the program will be executed in debug mode.

   Select the employee **Oindrilla** from the employee DropDownList and change the employee's address from **Kolkata** to Hyderabad as shown in the following figures:

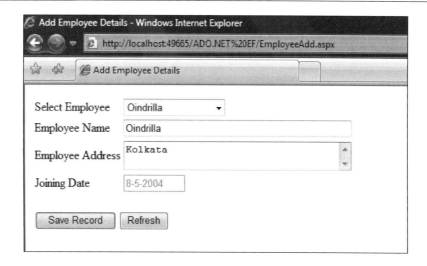

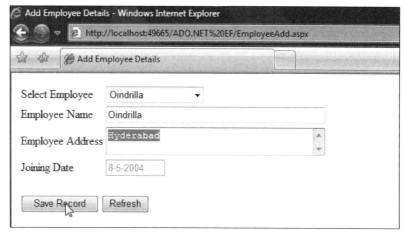

Working with the Object Services Layer

3. Now, click on **Save Record** to save these changes back to the database.

   The program breaks at the line where the break point has been set. Refer to the following figure:

```
int employeeID = int.Parse(drpEmployee.SelectedValue.Trim());
PayrollModel.PayrollEntities payrollEntities = new PayrollModel.PayrollEnti
try
{
    PayrollModel.EmployeeMaster employeeMaster =
    payrollEntities.EmployeeMaster.Where(emp => emp.EmployeeID == employeeI
    employeeMaster.EmployeeName = txtEmpName.Text.Trim();
    employeeMaster.EmployeeAddress = txtEmpAddress.Text.Trim();
    payrollEntities.SaveChanges();
    lblMessage.ForeColor = Color.Black;
    lblMessage.Text = "1 Record Saved";
}
catch (OptimisticConcurrencyException)
{
    lblMessage.ForeColor = Color.Red;
    lblMessage.Text = "Concurrency violation occurred..";
}
}

private void GetSelectedEmployeeDetails()
{
    int employeeID = int.Parse(drpEmployee.SelectedValue.Trim());
    PayrollDataContext dataContext = new PayrollDataContext();
    ObjectResult<PayrollModel.EmployeeMaster> result =
    dataContext.GetEmployeeRecords();

    foreach (PayrollModel.EmployeeMaster emp in result)
    {
        if (emp.EmployeeID == employeeID)
        {
```

4. Now, switch to the SQL Server Management Studio and execute the
   following statement to update the same record:

   Update Employee set EmployeeAddress = 'Chennai' where EmployeeID = 5

> You can use the `ToTraceString()` method on the `ObjectQuery`
> instance when using Object Services, or `EntityCommand` instance when
> using Entity Client, to retrieve the native SQL generated from the query
> as shown below:
>
>   ObjectQuery<Employee> query =
>   ctx.Employee.Where("it.EmployeeID = 1");
>   Console.WriteLine(query.ToTraceString());

The figure below shows the output once you execute the statement above in the SQL
Server Management Studio to update the record:

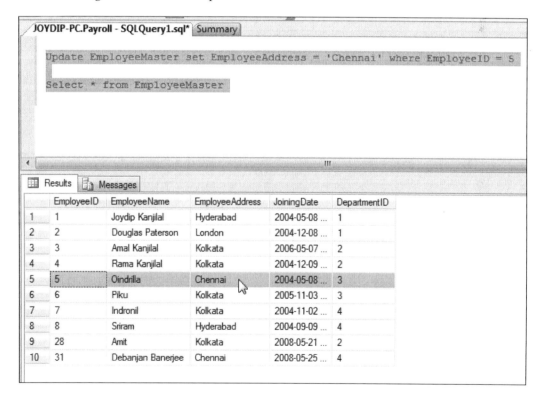

As you can see from the figure above, the `EmployeeAddress` of the employee
Oindrilla has been changed to **Chennai**.

Now, re-start the program execution by pressing *F5*. You will see the message **Concurrency violation occurred** being displayed as the SaveChanges method is called on the ObjectContext instance. The output is captured in the following screenshot:

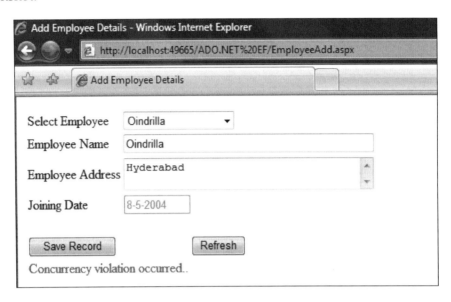

You can resolve the conflict by refreshing the ObjectContext instance before the changes are saved in the database. To do this, you need to call the Refresh method on the ObjectContext. However, remember that if you make a call to the Refresh method, even though the object's original values get updated, if the current values will be updated or not depends on the value of the RefreshMode property. To ensure that the objects are properly updated, you can call the Refresh () method with StoreWins after making a call to the SaveChanges () method on the ObjectContext instance.

Let's now incorporate the necessary change in the btnSave_Click event handler to resolve the conflict if one occurs. Here is the code:

```
protected void btnSave_Click(object sender, EventArgs e)
    {
        int employeeID = int.Parse(ddlEmployee.SelectedValue.Trim());
        PayrollModel.PayrollEntities ctx = new PayrollModel.PayrollEntities();
        PayrollModel.Employee employee = null;
        try
        {
            employee = ctx.Employee.Where
                (emp => emp.EmployeeID == employeeID).First();
```

Chapter 7

```
            employee.EmployeeName = txtEmpName.Text.Trim();
            employee.EmployeeAddress = txtEmpAddress.Text.Trim();
            ctx.SaveChanges();
            lblMessage.ForeColor = Color.Black;
            lblMessage.Text = "1 Record Saved";
        }
        catch (OptimisticConcurrencyException)
        {
            ctx.Refresh(RefreshMode.ClientWins, employee);
            lblMessage.ForeColor = Color.Green;
            lblMessage.Text = "Record saved after resolution of
                                                        conflict..";
        }
```

When you execute the application again, one of the following two scenarios can occur:

- If any conflict is detected, the Refresh method will be called on the ObjectContext instance, the conflict will be resolved, and the record saved in the database. The message **Record saved after resolution of conflict...** will be displayed in the lblMessage Label control as shown in the figure below:

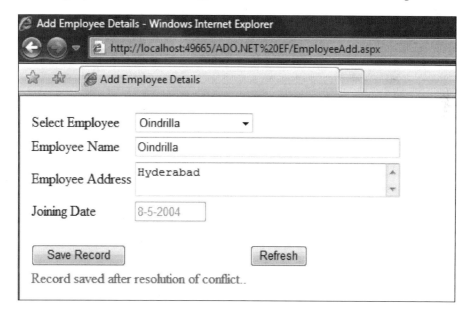

- If no conflict occurs, no OptimisticConcurrency exception will be thrown, the record will be saved, and the message **1 Record Saved.** will be displayed in the lblMessage Label control.

[175]

Inheritance in the Entity Framework

Inheritance is a property of Object-Oriented Programming which enables you to extend new classes from existing ones and provide additional functionality to them. Entity Framework supports the following types of inheritance:

- Table per hierarchy
- Table per type
- Table per concrete type

Table per Hierarchy

To implement Table per Hierarchy, or Single Table Inheritance, simply inherit a new class from your existing entity class and add the properties you need. As an example, suppose we need to create an entity called OldEmployee from the Employee entity in our Payroll EDM. To do this, create a new entity called OldEmployee in the designer and specify the base type as Employee. Here is how the two entities are represented in the EDM:

```xml
<EntityType Name="Employee">
        <Key>
          <PropertyRef Name="EmployeeID" />
        </Key>
        <Property Name="EmployeeID" Type="Int32" Nullable="false" />
        <Property Name="FirstName" Type="String" Nullable="false" MaxLength="50" Unicode="false" />
        <Property Name="LastName" Type="String" Nullable="false" MaxLength="50" Unicode="false" />
        <Property Name="Address" Type="String" Nullable="false" MaxLength="50" Unicode="false" />
        <Property Name="Phone" Type="String" Nullable="false" MaxLength="50" Unicode="false" />
        <Property Name="JoiningDate" Type="DateTime" Nullable="false" />
        <Property Name="LeavingDate" Type="DateTime" />
        <NavigationProperty Name="Department" Relationship="PayrollModel.FK_Employee_Department" FromRole="Employee" ToRole="Department" />
        <NavigationProperty Name="Designation" Relationship="PayrollModel.FK_Employee_Designation" FromRole="Employee" ToRole="Designation" />
        <NavigationProperty Name="ProvidentFund" Relationship="PayrollModel.FK_ProvidentFund_Employee" FromRole="Employee" ToRole="ProvidentFund" />
```

```xml
        <NavigationProperty Name="Salary" Relationship="PayrollModel
.FK_Salary_Employee" FromRole="Employee" ToRole="Salary" />
</EntityType>

<EntityType Name="OldEmployee" BaseType="PayrollModel.Employee" >
        <Property Name="ReasonOfLeaving" Type="String"
Nullable="true" MaxLength="50" Unicode="true" FixedLength="false" />
        <Property Name="HRComments" Type="String" Nullable="true"
MaxLength="50" Unicode="true" FixedLength="false" />
</EntityType>
```

And here is how the mapping information for these two entities in the EDM will be specified:

```xml
<EntityTypeMapping TypeName="IsTypeOf(PayrollModel.Employee)">
  <MappingFragment StoreEntitySet="Employee">
    <ScalarProperty Name="EmployeeID"
       ColumnName="EmployeeID" />
    <ScalarProperty Name="FirstName" ColumnName="FirstName" />
    <ScalarProperty Name="LastName" ColumnName="LastName" />
    <ScalarProperty Name="Address" ColumnName="Address" />
    <ScalarProperty Name="Phone" ColumnName="Phone" />
    <ScalarProperty Name="JoiningDate" ColumnName="JoiningDate" />
    <ScalarProperty Name="LeavingDate" ColumnName="LeavingDate" />
  </MappingFragment>
</EntityTypeMapping>

<EntityTypeMapping TypeName="OldEmployee">
  <TableMappingFragment TableName="Employee">
    <ScalarProperty Name="EmployeeID"
       ColumnName="EmployeeID" />
    <ScalarProperty Name="Reason" ColumnName="Reason" />
    <ScalarProperty Name="HRComments"
       ColumnName="HRComments" />
  </TableMappingFragment>
</EntityTypeMapping>
```

Table per Type

In this kind of inheritance, every type or entity are represented as tables in the database. The derived type has an associated BaseType from which it is derived. It is not, however, associated to any EntitySet in the EDM. In other words, in the Table per Type inheritance model, you define inheritance relationships in the EDM and store the data pertaining to each of these entities using their corresponding tables in the database.

Consider the Department entity declaration in the conceptual schema of the EDM as shown below:

```xml
<EntityType Name="Department">
 <Key>
    <PropertyRef Name="DepartmentID" />
 </Key>
 <Property Name="DepartmentID" Type="Int32" Nullable="false" />
 <Property Name="DepartmentName" Type="String" Nullable="false" MaxLength="50" Unicode="false" />
 <NavigationProperty Name="Employee" Relationship="PayrollModel.FK_Employee_Department" FromRole="Department" ToRole="Employee" />
</EntityType>
```

Here is how you can define a derived entity called `HREmployee` in the conceptual schema:

```xml
<EntityType Name="HRemployee" BaseType="PayrollModel.Department">
   <Property Name="NoOfEmployees" Type="Int32" Nullable="false" />
</EntityType>
```

In the SSDL section of the EDM, the two entities would then be represented as shown below:

```xml
<EntityType Name="Department">
    <Key>
      <PropertyRef Name="DepartmentID" />
    </Key>
    <Property Name="DepartmentID" Type="int" Nullable="false" StoreGeneratedPattern="Identity" />
    <Property Name="DepartmentName" Type="varchar" Nullable="false" MaxLength="50" />
</EntityType>
<EntityType Name="HRDepartment">
    <Key>
    <PropertyRef Name="HRDepartmentID" />
    </Key>
    <Property Name="NoOfEmployees" Type="int" Nullable="false" />
</EntityType>
```

Table per Concrete Type

In the Table per Concrete Type inheritance model, each table in our database represents the entity in its entirety. In essence, the individual tables contain the complete information of the entity. Therefore, you can simply load your entities directly from those tables. Here is how the mapping schema for your entities would look:

```xml
<EntityTypeMapping TypeName="IsTypeOf(PayrollModel.Employee)">
  <MappingFragment StoreEntitySet="Employee">
    <ScalarProperty Name="EmployeeID"
       ColumnName="EmployeeID" />
    <ScalarProperty Name="FirstName" ColumnName="FirstName" />
    <ScalarProperty Name="LastName" ColumnName="LastName" />
    <ScalarProperty Name="Address" ColumnName="Address" />
    <ScalarProperty Name="Phone" ColumnName="Phone" />
    <ScalarProperty Name="JoiningDate" ColumnName="JoiningDate" />
    <ScalarProperty Name="LeavingDate" ColumnName="LeavingDate" />
  </MappingFragment>
</EntityTypeMapping>

<EntityTypeMapping TypeName="OldEmployee">
 <TableMappingFragment TableName="OldEmployees">
    <ScalarProperty Name="EmployeeID" ColumnName="EmployeeID" />
    <ScalarProperty Name="FirstName" ColumnName="FirstName" />
    <ScalarProperty Name="LastName" ColumnName="LastName" />
    <ScalarProperty Name="LeavingDate"
    ColumnName="LeavingDate" />
    <ScalarProperty Name="Reason" ColumnName="Reason" />
    <ScalarProperty Name="HRComments"
       ColumnName="HRComments" />
  </TableMappingFragment>
</EntityTypeMapping>
```

> When you inherit from the `EntityObject` class to create your own custom entity types, ensure that the class and property names of the custom entity class match that of the entity type names and property names of the entity in the CSDL. The custom entity class should also contain a property for each property of the entity type defined in the CSDL.

Implementing Complex Types in the EDM

A complex type is actually a structures property. It can contain zero or more properties. To create a complex type, right-click on the design view mode of your EDM and create a new entity. Then, specify the properties you require. Here is how our complex type **Address** looks in the designer view:

And here is how the complex type Address is represented in the EDM:

```
<ComplexType Name="Address">
  <Property Name="Street" Type="String" />
  <Property Name="City" Type="String" />
  <Property Name="PinCode" Type="String" />
  <Property Name="Country" Type="String" />
  <Property Name="Phone" Type="String" />
</ComplexType>
```

Other entities, such as Employee, can then refer to this complex type in our EDM as shown below:

```
<EntityType Name="Employee">
        <Key>
          <PropertyRef Name="EmployeeID" />
        </Key>
        <Property Name="EmployeeID" Type="Int32" Nullable="false" />
        <Property Name="FirstName" Type="String" Nullable="false" MaxLength="50" Unicode="false" />
        <Property Name="LastName" Type="String" Nullable="false" MaxLength="50" Unicode="false" />
```

```
        <Property Name="Address" Type="PayrollModel.Address"
Nullable="false" MaxLength="50" Unicode="false" />
        <Property Name="Phone" Type="String" Nullable="false"
MaxLength="50" Unicode="false" />
        <Property Name="JoiningDate" Type="DateTime"
Nullable="false" />
        <Property Name="LeavingDate" Type="DateTime" />
</EntityType>
```

> To implement an abstract entity in the entity data model, we need to create an entity type in our Entity Data Model and set its Abstract flag to "true". Then, the code generator will automatically generate an abstract class that corresponds to this abstract type. Although the designer view requires that an abstract type should be mapped to a table, there is no such restriction imposed by the runtime, provided you are working with the generated CSDL, MSL, and SSDL files.

Summary

In this chapter, we discussed Object Services and how it can be used to perform CRUD operations against the Entity Data Model. We discussed how we can serialize and de-serialize an entity instance. We implemented a sample application that demonstrated how we can detect and resolve concurrency conflicts. We also discussed how we can extend, or inherit, new entities from existing ones and use them in our applications. In the next and final chapter of this book, we will take a look at ADO.NET Data Services and learn how we can use it with Entity Framework in our applications.

8
Introducing ADO.NET Data Services

ADO.NET Data Services, formerly known as Project Astoria, is comprised of a collection of patterns and libraries that can be used to expose an application's data as a service. This service can then be consumed by client applications using HTTP calls. You can use ADO.NET Data Services to isolate the Data Access Layer, and it exposes data via WCF services to discover, manipulate, and retrieve data in a corporate network. You can also use ADO.NET Data Services to expose data that is retrieved using the Entity Data Model as a service and then access this service using WCF service calls over HTTP protocol.

In this concluding chapter of the book, we will discuss the following:

- An overview of ADO.NET Data Services
- The REST-based model
- Creating an ADO.NET Data Service
- An overview of the System.Services.Data namespace
- Using the ADO.NET Data Services Client Library to perform CRUD operations and exposing Stored Procedures as URIs
- Exception Handling and Debugging ADO.NET Data Services
- Batching in ADO.NET Data Services to Improve Performance
- Consuming an ADO.NET Data Service Using LINQ

Introducing ADO.NET Data Services

Primarily designed in order to separate the presentation layer and data in a REST-based model, ADO.NET Data Services are used to expose data as a service so they can be accessed via HTTP requests. You can use the standard HTTP verbs MERGE, GET, POST, PUT, and DELETE and perform CRUD (Create, Read, Update and Delete) operations against the service. ADO.NET Data Services expose the database schema in terms of XML metadata. It uses Atom and JSON data formats for data transfer over the HTTP protocol.

ADO.NET Data Services isolate the Data Access Layer and expose data via WCF services. We do not need to have the presentation layer as a consumer of a Data Services. We could also have another service as in SOA scenarios.

You can use ADO.NET Data Services to expose data through web services in terms of EDM abstractions such as Entity Data Model (EDM) objects. These objects can then be accessed by any application in much the same way as a web service is accessed.

How Do ADO.NET Data Services and Web Services Differ?

The primary difference is that Web Services is based on SOAP and ADO.NET Data Services is based on a REST-model. While the former defines messages and exposes them, the latter defines resources and exposes them through URIs. Moreover, unlike using WSDL to define the endpoint of a service as in a Web Service, the REST-based model of ADO.NET Data Services uses the query string and the URL string to define the endpoint's URI. We will take a look at what the REST-based model is in the section that follows.

What is Representational State Transfer (REST)?

ADO.NET Data Services uses HTTP as its transport protocol and is based on a REST-model. In a REST-based model, the application's state and functionality is divided into resources. These are in turn addressable using URIs over HTTP. REST provides a stateless, client-server, and a cacheable model for data access. SOAP-based web service communication, which uses all web service protocols, is much heavier than REST-based ADO.NET Data Services.

The basic features of a REST-based architecture are:

- Resources are used to divide application state and its functionality.
- Resources share a uniform interface and are uniquely addressable.

The major benefits of a REST-based approach are as follows:

- Improved performance and response time
- Improved scalability
- Reduced KLOC at the client side
- Works on top of the HTTP protocol

Why Use ADO.NET Data Services?

The primary goal of ADO.NET Data Services is to create a REST-based model for exposing data services. REST is an architecture that is used in distributed hypermedia systems to transmit domain-specific data over the HTTP protocol. ADO.NET Data Services provides support for Optimistic Concurrency to detect data concurrency conflicts. It uses eTags, which are HTTP response headers in string format, to detect changes. These e-Tags, which are supported by HTTP 1.1, are used to denote the version or state of a resource. To know more on how concurrency is handled by ADO.NET Data Services, you can refer to the following website:

```
http://msdn.microsoft.com/en-us/library/cc668770.aspx
```

Features at a Glance

Here are some of the striking features of ADO.NET Data Services at a glance:

- Support for separation of data and presentation layers
- Support for REST model for exposing data as a service
- Facilitates creation of a uniform interface
- Model-based service contract

Using ADO.NET Data Services, you can declaratively specify the schema of the data. This includes creating the remote endpoints, automatically, and enabling paging and sorting of the exposed data without the need for writing any code. Moreover, if you are using ADO.NET Data Services to expose data retrieved through the Entity Data Model, these remote endpoints will also change accordingly when you change your Entity Data Model. Added to this, the REST-based model of ADO.NET Data Services provides you with a uniform interface to access data over HTTP regardless of the data that is exposed.

You can define the service operations and interceptors you are using which allow you to then define a method on the server that is identifiable using URIs. Next, you can call that method using the URI specified. You can use the interceptors to plug in your custom validation logic into the request/response pipeline. The best part of ADO.NET Data Services is that it uses HTTP entry points. In doing so, any HTTP client application can connect to it and perform CRUD operations.

Prerequisites

To work with ADO.NET Data Services, you should have the following installed on your system:

- Supported Operating Systems—Windows Server 2003, Windows Vista, or Windows XP
- Visual Studio 2008
- Visual Studio 2008 SP1 (this includes Entity Framework 1.0 and ADO.NET Data Services)
- Microsoft SQL Server 2005 or SQL Server Express
- ASP.NET Extensions CTP

Microsoft .NET Framework 3.5 SP1 and Visual Studio 2008 SP1 contain, among other things, ADO.NET Entity Framework v1, ADO.Net Data Services v1, and ASP.NET Dynamic Data. ADO.NET Data Services supports SQL Server 2008, MySQL, Oracle, and DB2 databases.

Exposing Data as a Service Using ADO.NET Data Services

You have two options to expose data as a service using ADO.NET Data Services:

- Use a relational database as the data source
- Use a data source other than a relational database

If you are using a relational database as the data source, you can use LINQ to SQL or Entity Framework to expose the data. On the other hand, you can use collections of objects as a data source too. In either case, you need to create an ADO.NET Data Service using the designer. In the next section, we will discuss how we can create an ADO.NET Data Service.

Chapter 8

Creating an ADO.NET Data Service

Here are the steps you should follow to create an ADO.NET Data Service to perform CRUD operations:

1. Open Visual Studio 2008.
2. Click on **File** and then **New - Project**.
3. Create a new ASP.NET Web Application from the list of the project templates displayed. This can be seen in the following figure.

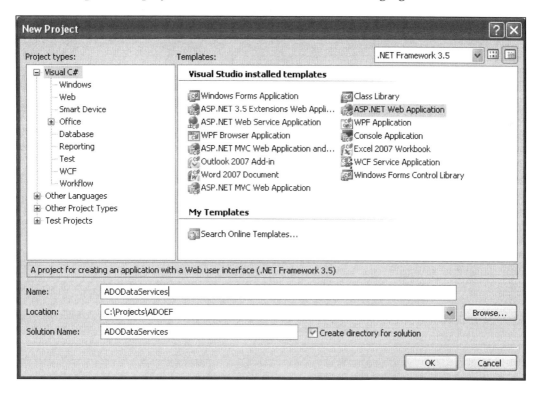

4. Right-click on the project in the solution explorer and choose **Add New Item**.

Introducing ADO.NET Data Services

5. Select ADO.NET Data Service from the list of the templates displayed and save it with a name as shown below:

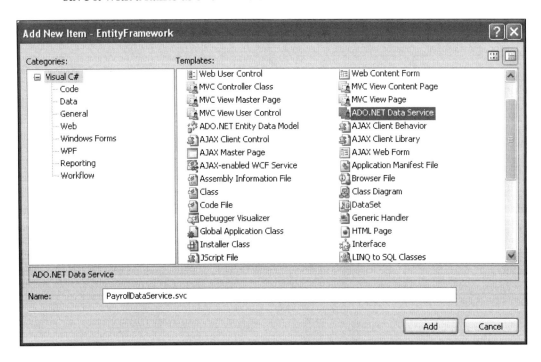

A `PayrollDataService` class is created and stored in the `PayrollDataService.svc.cs` file. Here is how the `PayrollDataService` class looks:

```
    public class PayrollDataService : DataService< /* TODO: put your data
    source class name here */ >
        {
            // This method is called once during service initialization to
allow
            // service-specific policies to be set
            public static void InitializeService(IDataServiceConfiguration
config)
            {
                // TODO: set rules to indicate which entity sets and
service operations are
                // visible, updatable, etc.
                // (for testing purposes use "*" to indicate all entity
sets/service
                // operations, but that option should NOT be used in
production systems)
                // Example for entity sets (this example uses "AllRead"
which allows reads but not writes)
```

```
            // config.SetResourceContainerAccessRule("MyEntityset",
ResourceContainerRights.AllRead);
            // Example for service operations
            // config.SetServiceOperationAccessRule
("MyServiceOperation", ServiceOperationRights.All);
        }
        // Query interceptors, change interceptors and service
operations go here
    }
```

Using a Relational Database as the Data Source

In this section, we will discuss how we can use ADO.NET Data Services to expose data retrieved through an Entity Data Model. Refer to the Payroll database and the Payroll Entity Data Model we created earlier in this book. Here are the steps to use a relational database as our data source

1. Create a new project called PayrollModel.
2. Create an Entity Data Model from the Payroll database following the same steps we discussed in Chapter 2. I will skip that discussion here.
3. Configure the Data Service

Now, you need to configure the `PayrollDataService` using the `InitializeService()` method to use the PayrollEntities data context. Here is what the class looks like now :

```
public class PayrollDataService : WebDataService< PayrollModel.
PayrollEntities >
    {
        public static void InitializeService
                            (IWebDataServiceConfiguration config)
        {
            // Example for entity sets (this example uses "AllRead"
which allows reads but not writes)
            config.SetEntitySetAccessRule("*",EntitySetRights.All);
        }
    }
```

As you can see from the `InitializeService()` method shown above, the `PayrollDataService` will allow you to read data, but you won't be able to insert, edit, or delete data using this data service. If you want to perform all operations, you can use the `ServiceOperationRights.All` option instead:

```
public class PayrollDataService : WebDataService< PayrollModel.
PayrollEntities >
    {
        public static void InitializeService
(IWebDataServiceConfiguration config)
        {
            // Example for service operations
            config.SetServiceOperationAccessRule("*",
ServiceOperationRights.All);
        }
    }
```

4. Execute the data service

Right-click on the data service file in the solution explorer and set it as the start page. Now, press *F5* to execute this data service. You are done!

Here is what the output looks like:

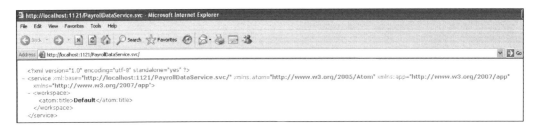

 You should turn off the Feed Reading View in Internet Explorer (IE) to view Atom (the default format returned by an ADO.NET Data Service). You can do this from the Content tab of Tools | Internet Options. Because IE 6 or earlier doesn't recognize the Atom content type, also ensure that you are using IE 7 or later.

You can also call this data service in the browser by using the URI as shown below:

`http://localhost:1121/PayrollDataService.svc`

Note that the port number used above is `1121` in my system as I have used the ASP.NET Development Server.

As you can see from the above output, the data service doesn't expose any of the entities by default. To do this, specify the following in the `InitializeService()` method to enable a read access to all the entities:

```
config.SetResourceContainerAccessRule("*", ResourceContainerRights.
AllRead);
```

When you execute the data service again, you can see the details of the entities listed as shown below:

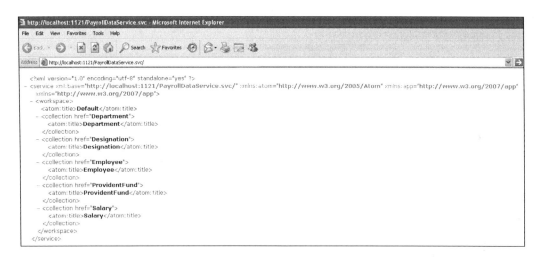

To return a list of all employees, use the following URI:

`http://localhost:1121/PayrollDataService.svc/Employee`

Here is what the output looks like in the web browser:

Introducing ADO.NET Data Services

Note that Atom and JSON are the formats used to represent and transfer the data. Further, the translation of a LINQ query to a corresponding HTTP request format is handled by the `DataServiceContext` class. Use the following URI in your web browser to retrieve the details of the employee whose Employee ID is 1:

`http://localhost:1121/PayrollDataService.svc/Employee(1)`

The output is shown below:

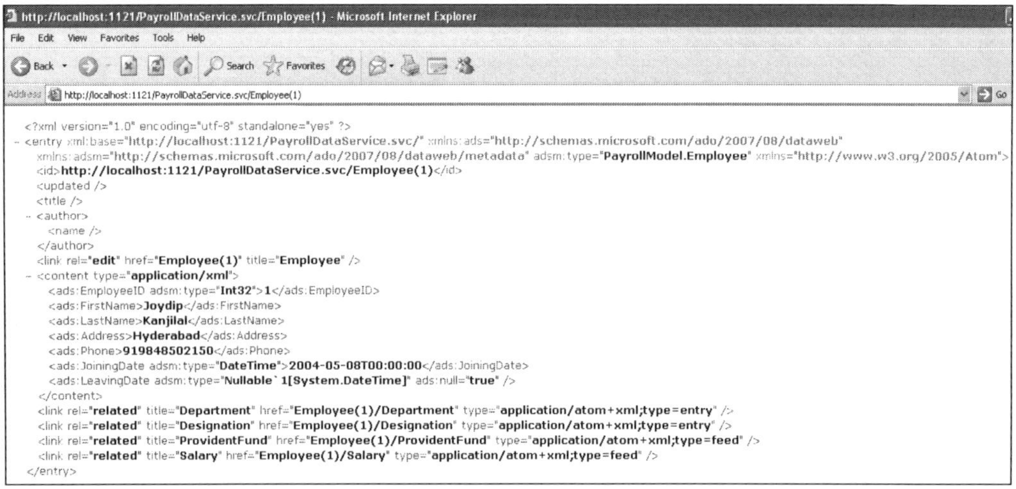

Using Data Sources Other Than a Relational Database

You can also use your data service to expose data retrieved from a custom collection class. Note that the class illustrated in the example below is a custom class, not the one we created earlier using the Entity Data Model. Here is an example:

```
[DataServiceKey("EmployeeID")]
    public class Employee
    {
        public int EmployeeID { get; set; }
        public string FirstName { get; set; }
        public string LastName { get; set; }
    }
    public class EmployeeData
    {
        static Employee[] employees;
        static EmployeeData()
```

```csharp
        {
            employees = new Employee[]
            {
              new Employee(){ EmployeeID=1, FirstName="Joydip", LastName = "Kanjilal"},
              new Employee(){ EmployeeID=1, FirstName="Douglas", LastName = "Paterson"},
              new Employee(){ EmployeeID=1, FirstName="Amal", LastName = "Kanjilal"},
              new Employee(){ EmployeeID=1, FirstName="Rama", LastName = "Kanjilal"},
              new Employee(){ EmployeeID=1, FirstName="Oindrilla", LastName = "RoyChowdhury"},
              new Employee(){ EmployeeID=1, FirstName="Soma", LastName = "RoyChowdhury"},
              new Employee(){ EmployeeID=1, FirstName="Indronil", LastName = "RoyChowdhury"},
              new Employee(){ EmployeeID=1, FirstName="Debanjan", LastName = "Banerjee"},
              new Employee(){ EmployeeID=1, FirstName="Tilak", LastName = "Tarafder"},
              new Employee(){ EmployeeID=1, FirstName="Sanjit", LastName = "Sil"},
              new Employee(){ EmployeeID=1, FirstName="Rakesh", LastName = "Gujjar"},
              new Employee(){ EmployeeID=1, FirstName="Sriram", LastName = "Putrevu"},
            };
        }
        public IQueryable<Employee> Employees
        {
            get { return employees.AsQueryable<Employee>(); }
        }
    }
```

Now, your data service should be referring to the `EmployeeData` class. Your data services should be exposing data retrieved from this class. Here is how the custom data service class should be represented:

```csharp
    public class EmployeeDataService : DataService<EmployeeData>
    {
        public static void InitializeService(IDataServiceConfiguration config)
        {
            config.SetEntitySetAccessRule("*", EntitySetRights.All);
        }
    }
```

Understanding the System.Services.Data Namespace

The `System.Services.Data` namespace is the core library for ADO.NET Data Services and provides access to it. In this section, we will take a look at the classes, interfaces, and enumerations in the `System.Services.Data` namespace. The following table lists the names and purposes of some of the important classes in the `System.Services.Data` namespace:

Class	Purpose
`DataService<T>`	This is the main entry point for developing a data service. This class serves as the base class for all data service classes.
`DataServiceHost`	This class is derived from `WebServiceHost` class and is used to instantiate a data service.
`DataServiceHostFactory`	This class is used to connect to Windows Communication Foundation from within a ADO.NET Data Service framework.
`DataServiceException`	This exception is thrown when there is an error accessing a data service from a client application.

The following table lists the names and purposes of the interfaces in the `System.Services.Data` namespace:

Interface	Purpose
`IUpdatable`	This is the interface that is used to insert or update data using an HTTP POST call.
`IRequestHandler`	This interface is used to provide access to controlling request messages.
`IDataServiceConfiguration`	This interface is used to set up the behavior of the data service.
`IDataServiceHost`	This interface is used to define the interactions between the data service and the environment on which the former has been hosted.
`IExpandProvider`	This interface defines the methods that are used to provide support for an expand query option.
`IExpandedResult`	This interface is used to provide support for the results that arise out of an expanded query option.

The following table lists the names and purposes of the enumeration in the `System.Services.Data` namespace:

Enumeration	Purpose
`UpdateOperations`	This represents the update operations that have been performed on an entity instance.
`EntitySetRights`	This represents the access rights to data exposed through an ADO.NET Data Service.
`ServiceOperationRights`	This represents the rights to service operations of an ADO.NET Data Service

The possible values for the `UpdateOperations` enumeration can be one of the following:

- `Add`
- `Change`
- `Delete`
- `None`

You can enable or disable access rights to a particular entity exposed through the data service using `EntitySetRights`. The possible values for `EntitySetRights` can be one of the following:

- `All`
- `AllRead`
- `AllWrite`
- `None`
- `ReadSingle`
- `ReadMultiple`
- `WriteInsert`
- `WriteUpdate`
- `WriteDelete`

The possible values for the `ServiceOperationRights` enumeration can be one of the following:

- `All`
- `AllRead`
- `None`
- `ReadSingle`
- `ReadMultiple`

Introducing ADO.NET Data Services

Restricting Access to Resources

A data service doesn't expose any of its resources by default. There is also no read or write access to resources. You need to explicitly enable the resources and provide read/write accesses to them.

To provide access to resources in a data service, you need to use the `InitializeService()` method. The following code snippet illustrates how you can enable access to all the resources of our `PayrollDataService` with all operations permitted:

```
public class PayrollDataService : WebDataService <PayrollModel.PayrollEntities>
    {
        public static void InitializeService(IDataServiceConfiguration
                    config)
        {
            config.SetEntitySetAccessRule("*", EntitySetRights.All);
        }
    }
```

The following code snippet illustrates how you can use the `InitializeService()` method to restrict access to the Employee, Department, and Salary entities:

```
public class PayrollDataService : WebDataService <PayrollModel.PayrollEntities>
    {
        public static void InitializeService
(IDataServiceConfiguration  config)
        {
            config.SetEntitySetAccessRule("Employee",
                                        EntitySetRights.All);
            config.SetEntitySetAccessRule("Department",
 EntitySetRights.WriteInsert | EntitySetRights.WriteUpdate);
            config.SetEntitySetAccessRule("Salary",
                                        EntitySetRights.All);
        }
    }
```

As you can see from the code snippet above three entities have been exposed through the data service. All operations have been enabled in the Employee and Salary entities, but only insert and update operations are possible in the Department entity. You cannot delete a Department record using the data service shown above.

You can also enable access to one record at a time for a particular entity exposed through the data service. Here is how you can do this:

```
public class PayrollDataService : WebDataService <PayrollModel.
PayrollEntities>
    {
        public static void InitializeService
(IDataServiceConfiguration  config)
        {
            config.SetEntitySetAccessRule("Employee", EntitySetRights.
ReadSingle);
        }
    }
```

Working with the ADO.NET Data Service Client Library

ADO.NET Data Services includes a powerful client library that provides a programming model that you can use to perform CRUD operations in your applications. To use the ADO.NET Client Library, you need to include the `System.Data.Services.Client` namespace in your program. Note that the ADO.NET Client Library is accessible from any client application including Windows Forms, Web Forms, WPF, etc. The two major classes included in this library are the `DataServiceContext` class and the `DataServiceQuery` class. While the former represents the runtime context of the data service, the latter represents the query against the store.

To start using the ADO.NET Data Service Client, ensure that you add a reference to the `System.Data.Services.Client` assembly to your project. See this in the following figure:

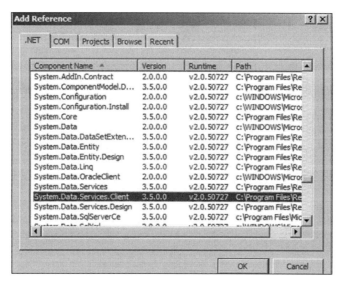

Introducing ADO.NET Data Services

Generating the Client-Side Entity Classes

To generate the client-side entity classes, follow these steps:

1. Open a command window and switch to the following folder:
   `C:\WINDOWS\Microsoft.NET\Framework\v3.5`

2. Now, type the following in the command prompt to generate the client side entity classes:
   `datasvcutil.exe /uri:http://localhost:1156/PayrollDataService.svc /out:PayrollEntities.cs`

The command above will query the metadata of the data service and then generate the appropriate entity classes in the file specified.

Inserting a Record

The following code snippet illustrates how you can use this library to insert data:

```
using System;
using System.Data.Services.Client;
using System.Linq;
using PayrollModel;

namespace ADODataServiceTest
{
    class Program
    {
        static void Main(string[] args)
        {
            DataServiceContext dataServiceContext = new
               DataServiceContext(new
                                   Uri("http://localhost:1156/
PayrollDataService.svc"));
            dataServiceContext.MergeOption = MergeOption.AppendOnly;
            Department department = new Department();
            department.DepartmentName = "Sales";
            dataServiceContext.AddObject("Department", department);
            dataServiceContext.SaveChanges();
        }
    }
}
```

The `MergeOption` enumeration in the `System.Data.Objects` namespace is used to specifiy the way in which the objects that have been loaded into the Object Context are merged with the ones that are already available in the Object Context. Referring to the code snippet above, note that as you are inserting a record, you should specify the `MergeOption` of the `DataService` as `AppendOnly`. Here is a list of the possible values of `MergeOption`:

- `AppendOnly`: This is the default option and is used to append new entities. Note that existing entities will not be modified.
- `NoTracking`: When set, this will ensure that the `ObjectStateManager` is not changed.
- `OverwriteChanges`: Used to overwrite the current values in the `ObjectStateEntry` with the most recent values from the store.
- `PreserveChanges`: Used to replace the original values without changing the current ones.

Updating a Record

To update data using the ADO.NET Data Services Client, you can use the following code:

```
using System;
using System.Data.Services.Client;
using System.Linq;
using PayrollModel;
namespace ADODataServiceTest
{
    class Program
    {
        static void Main(string[] args)
        {
            DataServiceContext dataServiceContext = new
                DataServiceContext(new
                            Uri("http://localhost:1156/
PayrollDataService.svc"));
            var record = (from d in dataServiceContext.Department
                    where d.DepartmentName == "Sales"
                    select d).First();
            record.DepartmentName = "Marketing";
            dataServiceContext.AddObject("Department", record);
            dataServiceContext.SaveChanges();
        }
    }
}
```

> **Data Binding Using a Data Service**
>
> DataServiceContext ctx = new DataServiceContext (new Uri (`http://localhost:1156/PayrollDataService.svc`));
>
> DataServiceQuery<Employee> employee = ctx.CreateQuery<Employee>("/Employee?orderby=LastName");
>
> Repeater1.DataSource = employees;
>
> Repeater1.DataBind();

Deleting a Record

To delete a record using the ADO.NET Data Services Client, you can use the following code:

```
using System;
using System.Data.Services.Client;
using System.Linq;
using PayrollModel;

namespace ADODataServiceTest
{
    class Program
    {
        static void Main(string[] args)
        {
            DataServiceContext dataServiceContext = new
              DataServiceContext(new
                            Uri("http://localhost:1156/
PayrollDataService.svc"));
            var record = (from d in dataServiceContext.Department
                    where d.DepartmentName == "Sales"
                    select d).First();

            dataServiceContext.DeleteObject("Department", record);
            dataServiceContext.SaveChanges();
        }
    }
}
```

Consuming an ADO.NET Data Service Using LINQ

The `DataService` class enables you to execute LINQ queries against an ADO.NET Data Service. In other words, you can also consume an ADO.NET Data Service using LINQ. Here is an example that illustrates how you can use LINQ to retrieve the details of all employees who live in Hyderabad:

```
using System;
using System.Data.Services.Client;
using System.Linq;
using PayrollModel;
namespace ConsumeService
{
    class Program
    {
        static void Main(string[] args)
        {
            PayrollEntities ctx = new
                    PayrollEntities("http://localhost:1156/
PayrollDataService.svc ");
            ctx.MergeOption = MergeOption.AppendOnly;
            var data = from emp in ctx.Employee
                       where emp.Address == "Hyderabad"
                       select emp;
            foreach (var employee in data)
            {
                Console.WriteLine(employee.FirstName+"  "+ employee.LastName);
            }
        }
    }
}
```

Exposing a Stored Procedure as a URI

To expose a stored procedure as a URI, follow these steps:

1. Define a `GetData()` method on your `DataService` class using the `WebGet` attribute.
2. Now, call a method on your `ObjectContext` from this method.

Introducing ADO.NET Data Services

Here is an example:

```
public class PayrollDataService : DataService<PayrollModel.
PayrollEntities>
{
public static void InitializeService(IDataServiceConfiguration config)
  {
        // Entity sets access configuration.
          config.SetEntitySetAccessRule("*", EntitySetRights.AllRead);

        // Service operations access configuration.
          config.SetServiceOperationAccessRule
("GetEmployeesByDesignation",
                    ServiceOperationRights.All);
  }

    [WebGet]

    public IQueryable<Orders> GetEmployeesByDesignation(string
designationName)
    {
      return ((PayrollModel.PayrollEntities)this.CurrentDataSource).
EmployeesByDesignation(designationName).AsQueryable();
    }
}
```

In the example above, the data service class `PayrollDataService` extends the `DataService` class of the ADO.NET Data Services library. The `PayrollEntities` class is our custom `ObjectContext` class. You can now invoke this service operation as shown below:

```
http://PayrollDataService.svc/GetEmployeesByDesignation?
designationName='Manager'
```

> The `WebClient` code generator doesn't generate functions for using stored procedures. If you want to use stored procedures, you should use `WebGet` or `WebInvoke` functions in your service class.

Handling Exceptions in ADO.NET Data Services

There may be many situations where a data service call might fail. Any error that is raised in the data service should be represented in the form of `DataServiceException` in order to transfer a structured error to the client. The following code example illustrates how to change our custom data service class to handle exceptions:

```
public class PayrollDataService : WebDataService <PayrollModel.
PayrollEntities>
    {
        public static void InitializeService
(IDataServiceConfiguration  config)
        {
             config.SetEntitySetAccessRule("*", EntitySetRights.All);
             config.UseVerboseErrors = false;
        }
    protected override void HandleException(HandleExceptionArgs args)
        {
          if(args.Exception is ArgumentException)
            {
                ArgumentException ex =
                              (ArgumentException) args.Exception;
                args.Exception = new DataServiceException(400,
                «PropertySyntaxError:» + ex.ParamName,
                "Error Message: ", "en-US", ex);
            }
        }
    }
```

> ### Handling a DataServiceQuery Exception at the Client Application
>
> Suppose a DataServiceQuery exception has been thrown to the client as a result of a DataServiceException at the server. Here is how you can trap the exception at the client side and get the InnerException message:
>
>
>
> ```
>     try
>     {
>       //some code
>     }
>     catch (DataServiceQueryException ex)
>     {
>         QueryOperationResponse response = ex.Response;
>         Console.WriteLine("The error message is: "+response.Error.Message);
>         Console.WriteLine("The error code is: "+response.StatusCode);
>     }
> ```

Batching ADO.NET Data Services Requests to Improve Performance

Batching is a feature that facilitates sending HTTP requests in a batch so that the number of round trips to the server are reduced and the consumer of the data service's performance is increased. To use this feature, use a method called `ExecuteBatch` that accepts one of more `DataServiceRequest` instances as a parameter. Here is an example:

```
var dataServiceProxy = new PayrollDataContext(new Uri("http://
localhost:1156/PayrollDataService.svc"));
dataServiceProxy.MergeOption = MergeOption.AppendOnly;
var employees = from emp in dataServiceProxy.Employee select emp;
var employeesUri = new Uri(employees.ToString());
var departments = from dept in dataServiceProxy.Department select
dept;
var departmentsUri = new Uri(departments.ToString());
var result = dataServiceProxy.ExecuteBatch(
    new DataServiceRequest<Employee>(employeesUri),
    new DataServiceRequest<Department>(departmentsUri));
foreach (var r in result)
{
     QueryOperationResponse queryOperationResponse = r as
QueryOperationResponse;
     if (null !=  queryResponse)
     {
        foreach (var e in queryOperationResponse.OfType<Employee>())
        {
           Console.WriteLine(e.FirstName + " "+ e.LastName);
        }
     }
}
```

You can also use batching in the `SaveChanges` method for inserts, updates, or deletes so that all changes are submitted together. The following code snippet demonstrates this:

```
dataServiceProxy.SaveChanges(SaveChangesOptions.Batch);
```

Debugging Your Data Service

You might run into problems when accessing ADO.NET Data Service from a client application for some reason or another. A normal error message you will get is similar to the following:

```xml
<?xml version="1.0" encoding="utf-8" standalone="yes"?>
<error xmlns="http://schemas.microsoft.com/ado/2007/08/dataservices/
metadata">
  <code></code>
  <message xml:lang="en-US">An error occurred while processing this request.</message>
</error>
```

As you can see from the code snippet above the details of the error are not displayed and as such, it would be difficult to debug the cause of the error. In such situations, you should set `UseVerboseErrors` to `true` in the `ServiceConfiguration` of your data service and also configure your `ServiceBehavior` using the `IncludeExceptionDetailInFaults` attribute as shown below:

```
[System.ServiceModel.ServiceBehavior(IncludeExceptionDetailInFaults = true)]
public class PayrollDataService : WebDataService<PayrollEntities>
    {
        public static void InitializeService (IWebDataServiceConfiguration config)
        {
            config.UseVerboseErrors = true;
            config.SetEntitySetAccessRule("*", EntitySetRights.All);
        }
    }
```

References

Here is a list of the links to some great resources on ADO.NET Data Services and REST:

http://msdn.microsoft.com/en-us/library/cc668808.aspx

http://www.microsoft.com/uk/msdn/screencasts/

http://msdn.microsoft.com/en-us/library/cc668767.aspx

http://msdn.microsoft.com/en-us/library/cc716655.aspx

http://msdn.microsoft.com/en-us/library/cc668775.aspx

http://blogs.msdn.com/astoriateam/default.aspx

http://reddevnews.com/techbriefs/article.aspx?editorialsid=1069

http://oakleafblog.blogspot.com/

http://blogs.msdn.com/astoriateam/archive/2008/04/22/optimistic-concurrency-data-services.aspx

Summary

ADO.NET Data Services are great in the sense that you can expose your application's data as a service. You can then consume it from any application that has support for performing HTTP requests to perform CRUD operations seamlessly. In this chapter, we have had a quick tour of ADO.NET Data Services including its features and benefits. We have also seen the REST-based model of ADO.NET Data Services, and how we can integrate ADO.NET Data Services with the ADO.NET Entity Framework. We have also discussed how to use ADO.NET Data Services to expose data retrieved through an Entity Data Model as a service so that it can be consumed by client applications. We also discussed how to handle exceptions and debug errors that might occur as a result of accessing a data service. This ends our journey towards mastering the ADO.NET Entity Framework. Happy reading!

Index

A

abstract entity, implementing in EDM 181
ADO.NET Data Service Client Library
  client side entity classes, generating 198
  record, deleting 200
  record, inserting 198
  record, updating 199
  working with 197
ADO.NET Data Service requests
  batching 204
  data service, debugging 204, 205
ADO.NET Data Services
  about 184
  access, restricting to resources 196, 197
  and web services, differentiating 184
  Client Library, working with 197
  consuming, LINQ used 201
  exceptions, handling 202, 203
  features 185
  need for 185
  prerequisites 186
  references 205
  REST based 184
  stored procedure, exposing as URI 201, 202
  system.services.data namespace 194
ADO.NET Data Services, data exposing as service
  creating 187-189
  other data source, using 192, 193
  relational database, using as data source 189-192
ADO.NET Entity Client, working with
  about 116
  connection, closing 121, 122
  connection, opening 118
  connection string, building 117
  entity connection, creating 118
  queries executing, entity command used 119-121
ADO.NET Entity Data Model. *See* **EDM**
ADO.NET entity data source control 51-53
ADO.NET Entity Framework
  about 9
  application implementing, EDM used 54-56
  application implementing, entity data model used 54, 56
  benefits 19
  components 10
  features 19
  layers 10
  prerequisites, installing 20
ADO.NET Entity Framework and ORM tools, differentiating 9

B

batching
  ADO.NET Data Service requests 204

C

canonical functions, Entity SQL
  aggregate functions 113, 114
  bitwise functions 114
  categories 113
  date functions 115
  mathematical functions 113
  string functions 114
  time functions 115
categories, Entity SQL
  collection 111

reference 112
row 111
change tracking, entity framework
  concurrency conflicts 161
  concurrency conflicts, handling 170
  custom DataContext,
      implementing 164-166
  data concurrencies, handling ways 162
  data concurrencies, optimistic mode 162
  data concurrencies, pessimistic mode 162
  form, creating 162-164
  sample application, implementing 162
complex type, implementing in EDM 180
components, ADO.NET Entity Framework
  entity client 16
  Entity Data Model (EDM) 10, 11
  entity SQL 16, 17
  Language Integrated Query (LINQ) to
      Entities 16
  object model (O-Space) 15
  object services 18, 19
**Conceptual Schema Definition Language
  (CSDL schema) 69, 70, 75**

D

data, exposing as services
  ADO.NET Data Services used 186
data, querying
  LINQ to Entities used 131
  LINQ used 140, 142
DataContexts 130
data model 8
data paging, Entity SQL 115
**DataServiceQuery exception, handling
  at client application 203**
DLINQ 129

E

E-SQL. *See* Entity SQL
EDM
  about 10
  abstract entity, implementing 181
  AssociationSet, defining 62
  C-S mapping layer 12
  complex type, implementing 180
  conceptual layer or C-Space layer 12

containment, defining 63
creating 37
diagrammatic representation 12
EntityContainer, defining 63, 64
EntitySet, defining 60, 61
existing entity type, extending 61, 62
fitting in 11
layers 12
logical or storage layer 12
multiplicity, defining 63
payroll EDM 64
payroll EDM, layers 68, 69, 83, 84
representing 13
S-Space 12
stored procedures, mapping that return
    custom entity types 101, 102
stored procedures, mapping to functions
    85, 86, 87, 88, 89
stored procedures, mapping with no entity
    set 99
EDM, creating
  ADO.NET entity data model designer used
      38-47
  EdmGen tool used 47-51
entity 35
  about 60
  EntityKey 60
  EntityType 60
  model browser 67
entity client 16
Entity Data Model. *See* EDM
entity data source control 51-53
entity framework
  inheritance 176
entity instances
  de-serializing, ObjectContext used 160, 161
  serializing, ObjectContext used 159, 160
entity model browser 67, 68
Entity SQL
  about 16, 17
  canonical functions 113
  categories 111
  complex joins, avoiding 17
  data paging 115
  expressions 109
  features 105
  identifiers 110

[208]

LINQ to Entities 105
operators 106
other operations 123
overview 104
transact SQL (T-SQL) to entity SQL (E-SQL) 104, 105
types 111
variables 111
Entity SQL language. *See* **Entity SQL**
exceptions, handling 202, 203
expressions, Entity SQL
query expressions 109
expressions, LINQ to Entities
about 143
comparision expressions 144, 145
constant expressions 144
immediate and defered query execution 148-150
initializing expressions 145
navigation properties 147, 148
null comparisons 146
queries, compiling 150

F

features, ADO.NET Entity Framework 19

G

grouping, LINQ operators 134

I

identifiers, Entity SQL
quoted identifiers 110
simple identifiers 110
inheritance, entity framework
single table inheritance 176, 177
table per concrete type, implementing 179
table per hierarchy, implementing 176, 177
table per type, implementing 177-179
installing, ADO.NET Entity Framework
software, downloading 20, 21
software, installing 21-29

J

joining, LINQ operators 134

L

Language Integrated Query. *See* **LINQ**
Language Integrated Query (LINQ) to Entities 16
layers, ADO.NET Entity Framework 10
LINQ
about 127, 128
architecture 128
data, querying 140, 142
need for 128
operators 133
LINQ architecture
about 128
LINQ to Entities 131
LINQ to Entities and LINQ to SQL, differences 132
LINQ to Objects 130, 131
LINQ to SQL 129, 130
LINQ to XML 129
LINQ to Entities
about 131
and ADO.NET entity framework, relating 132
and entity framework 131
data, querying 131
expressions 143
LINQ to Objects 130, 131
LINQ to SQL 129, 130
LINQ to XML 129
logical model 35

M

MSL schema 82, 84

O

object
adding, to ObjectContext 157
attaching 158
deleting 157
detaching 159
modifying 157
object model 8, 35
object model (O-Space) 15
object services
about 18, 19, 151

[209]

data, querying 156
features 153
object services layer. *See* **object services**
operations, Entity SQL
  native SQL, retrieving from
      EntityCommand 124
  record inserting, Entity SQL used 123
  record inserting, with foreign key
      constraint 124
  transaction management 125, 126
operators, Entity SQL
  arithmetic operators 106
  categories 106
  comparision operators 107
  logical operators 107
  operator precedence 109
  reference operators 108
  set operators 108
  type operators 108
operators, LINQ
  about 133
  aggregation 133, 136
  concatenation 133
  conversion 134, 138, 139
  element 134, 139
  equality 134
  generation 134
  grouping 134
  joining 134
  ordering 135, 137
  partitioning 135
  projection 135, 136
  quantifiers 135-138
  restriction 135-138
  set 135, 139

P

payroll database, designing 29-34
payroll entity data model (EDM)
  Conceptual Schema Definition Language
      (CSDL) schema 69-75
  design view 64
  entity data model, layers 68
  entity model browser 67, 68
  mapping details, window 65, 66
  MSL schema 82-84
  ObjectContext class 153-156
  SSDL schema 75-80
prerequisites, installing 20

Q

query expressions, Entity SQL 109

R

references, ADO.NET Data Services 205
relational model 35
Representational State Transfer. *See* **REST**
REST
  benefits 185
  features 185

S

SSDL schema 75, 76, 80
stored procedures, EDM
  association sets, mapping 93-99
  create function, mapping to entities 89-92
  CUD function, mapping to entities 89-92
  delete function, mapping to entities 89-92
  mapping, that return custom entity types
      101, 102
  mapping, with no entity sets 99
  mapping to functions, in EDM 85-89
  update function, mapping to entities 89-92
  using 100
system.services.data namespace
  classes, purpose 194
  enumeration 195
  enumeration, purpose 195
  interfaces 194
  interfaces, purpose 194

T

types, Entity SQL 111

V

variables, Entity SQL 111

X

XLINQ 129

Thank you for buying
Entity Framework Tutorial

About Packt Publishing

Packt, pronounced 'packed', published its first book "*Mastering phpMyAdmin for Effective MySQL Management*" in April 2004 and subsequently continued to specialize in publishing highly focused books on specific technologies and solutions.

Our books and publications share the experiences of your fellow IT professionals in adapting and customizing today's systems, applications, and frameworks. Our solution based books give you the knowledge and power to customize the software and technologies you're using to get the job done. Packt books are more specific and less general than the IT books you have seen in the past. Our unique business model allows us to bring you more focused information, giving you more of what you need to know, and less of what you don't.

Packt is a modern, yet unique publishing company, which focuses on producing quality, cutting-edge books for communities of developers, administrators, and newbies alike. For more information, please visit our website: `www.packtpub.com`.

Writing for Packt

We welcome all inquiries from people who are interested in authoring. Book proposals should be sent to `author@packtpub.com`. If your book idea is still at an early stage and you would like to discuss it first before writing a formal book proposal, contact us; one of our commissioning editors will get in touch with you.

We're not just looking for published authors; if you have strong technical skills but no writing experience, our experienced editors can help you develop a writing career, or simply get some additional reward for your expertise.

ODP.NET Developer's Guide
ISBN: 978-1-847191-96-0   Paperback: 300 pages

A practical guide for developers working with the Oracle Data Provider for .NET and the Oracle Developer Tools for Visual Studio 2005

1. Application development with ODP.NET
2. Dealing with XML DB using ODP.NET
3. Oracle Developer Tools for Visual Studio .NET

ASP.NET 3.5 Application Architecture and Design
ISBN: 978-1-847195-50-0   Paperback: 260 pages

Build robust, scalable ASP.NET applications quickly and easily

1. Master the architectural options in ASP.NET to enhance your applications
2. Develop and implement n-tier architecture to allow you to modify a component without disturbing the next one
3. Design scalable and maintainable web applications rapidly
4. Implement ASP.NET MVC framework to manage various components independently

Please check **www.PacktPub.com** for information on our titles

SharePoint Designer Tutorial

ISBN: 9978-1-847194-42-8　　　Paperback: 170 pages

Get started with SharePoint Designer and learn to put together a business website with SharePoint

1. Become comfortable in the SharePoint Designer environment
2. Learn about SharePoint Designer features as you create a SharePoint website
3. Step-by-step instructions and careful explanations

ASP.NET 3.5 Social Networking

ISBN: 978-1-847194-78-7　　　Paperback: 613 pages

An expert guide to building enterprise-ready social networking and community applications with ASP.NET 3.5

1. Create a full-featured, enterprise-grade social network using ASP.NET 3.5
2. Learn key new ASP.NET topics in a practical, hands-on way: LINQ, AJAX, C# 3.0, n-tier architectures, and MVC
3. Build friends lists, messaging systems, user profiles, blogs, message boards, groups, and more
4. Rich with example code, clear explanations, interesting examples, and practical advice – a truly hands-on book for ASP.NET developers

Please check **www.PacktPub.com** for information on our titles